LAWS
—of the—
HEART

While this book is intended for the reader's personal enjoyment and profit, it is also designed for group study. A personal and group study guide is included at the end of the text.

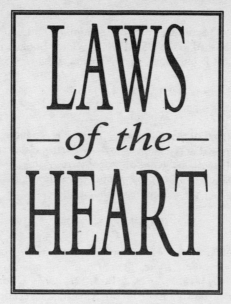

LAWS
—of the—
HEART

10 Essentials of a Liberated Life

BILL HYBELS

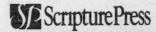

Raans Road, Amersham on-the-Hill, Bucks HP6 6JQ, England

ISBN 1 872059 87 2

Production and Printing in England for
SCRIPTURE PRESS FOUNDATION (UK) LTD
Raans Road, Amersham on-the-Hill, Bucks HP6 6JQ by
Nuprint Ltd, Station Road, Harpenden, AL5 4SE.

Contents

Introduction

One   CHOOSE THE LIVING GOD   *7*

Two   DON'T SETTLE FOR SHADOWS   *19*

Three   TURN PROFANITY INTO PRAISE   *30*

Four   FOLLOW THE MAINTENANCE SCHEDULE   *42*

Five   FULFILL THE CYCLE OF LOVE   *52*

Six   DESTROY THE KILLER IN YOU   *64*

Seven   KEEP PLEASURE UNDEFILED   *72*

Eight   ACQUIRE BY THE RULES   *83*

Nine   HOLD TO THE TRUTH   *95*

Ten   CRAVE CONTENTMENT   *107*

One
Choose the Living God

"You shall have no other gods before Me" (Exodus 20:3).

Born into a staunch Dutch Christian Reformed family, I developed the habit of regular church attendance at an early age. Neither threatening weather conditions, tight schedules, nor difficult circumstances would excuse my three sisters, my brother, or me from our usual places in the pew between Mom and Dad.

As is true in most Christian Reformed churches, there came a point in every Sunday morning service when my pastor took on a particularly grave appearance. In a voice that seemed to possess an almost unearthly quality, he'd announce, "And now, beloved, hear the reading of the Law of God."

As he paused to open the pulpit Bible, we readjusted our positions in the pew, and prepared for his lengthy discourse. He continued, "And God spake all these words saying, 'I am the Lord thy God, which have brought thee out of the land of Egypt, out of the house of bondage. Thou shalt have no other gods before Me' " (Ex. 20:2, KJV). When he concluded his reading of Exodus 20—the chapter which contains the Ten Commandments—he read the New Testament summary of the Law:

7

"Thou shalt love the Lord thy God with all thy heart, and with all thy soul, and with all thy mind. . . . And . . . thy neighbor as thyself" (Matt. 22:37-39, KJV).Then, in the same solemn tone, he'd proclaim: "Thus endeth the reading of the Law."

As a child, I had a difficult time coping with this weekly ritual. I always knew exactly what the minister was going to say—in fact, I could have recited the entire passage along with him—so I felt no need to hear it again. Putting my mind on autopilot, I simply endured the repetitious reading without ever considering its real meaning. All I gained from this youthful exercise in endurance was a memorized list of scriptural do's and don'ts.

On the brighter side, though, the experience provided me with a greater knowledge of the Ten Commandments than many adults possess. *Newsweek* magazine once reported that only 49 percent of all Protestants, and 44 percent of all Roman Catholics, could name even *four* of the Ten Commandments! In a seminary class I once taught, I referred to Exodus 20 and casually remarked, "Of course, you all know the Ten Commandments." The empty looks on my students' faces failed to convince me that they did. So I asked if someone—anyone—could name the first commandment. In a class of second-year seminary students, not one student could recite the first commandment!

I continued to prod until one student finally recited the Matthew 22 summary, and from there we backed up to the first commandment. After five or six minutes of painstaking persistence, I managed to pull six of the Ten Commandments from the minds of those future Christian leaders.

My purpose in writing this book is not merely to provide an easy-to-memorize list of the Ten Commandments, though most Christians probably would do well to begin there. Rather, my aim is to show Christians that these famous commands, though given by God centuries ago, have something very important to say to us *today*. They still have the power to touch our inner lives, and to liberate us from the vices that enslave us and the sins that destroy us.

Moses received these commandments three months after

God miraculously delivered the nation of Israel from the land of Egypt. The Lord called Moses to the top of Mount Sinai, gave him the commandments during a spectacular display of thunder, lightning, smoke, and trumpet sounds (Ex. 19:16-19), and then sent him back to the people with the commandments etched on tablets of stone.

The first four commandments, or the First Table, taught the people how to relate to God. The fifth through tenth commandments, the Second Table, taught them how to relate to one another. If we are willing to take these instructions seriously, they can teach us the same lessons today.

Words of Wisdom

"You shall have no other gods before Me" (Ex. 20:3). With these words, the Almighty God of the Israelites established His rightful position of preeminence. In a historical setting that encouraged devotion to many gods, the God of Israel demanded a single-minded allegiance — to Himself.

Undoubtedly, many of the Israelites questioned Moses on this point, just as some persons question this commandment today. "Was God nervous?" they ask. "Did the competition threaten Him? Why did He have to be so exclusive?"

Those of us who *do* give our allegiance to the God of the Old Testament would never frame our questions in such blunt terms. But still, we too wonder, "Why did God say this? What were His motives?"

One thing of which we can be sure is that God had good reasons for giving this commandment. The Lord tells us specifically that His commands are never burdensome (1 John 5:3). By this, He doesn't necessarily mean they're easy to keep. Rather, He's telling us that they're never foolish. They are never unnecessary or purely arbitrary. He doesn't force us to observe meaningless formalities, nor does He impose rules that have no value.

On the contrary, every guideline, every law, every imperative in the Bible was crafted in infinite wisdom. They were given not only to honor God, but to benefit us as well. The entire Book of Deuteronomy, for example, is a testament to this truth. In that book Moses repeatedly states that God gave the commandments for our good and promises to bless us if we obey them.

We can never know all that was in God's mind when He gave the first commandment. We can, however, make some educated assumptions, for certain obvious truths give us at least a partial glimpse of His motivation.

Only God Is Worthy

First, God seems to be telling us that no other being in the universe is worthy of our worship. Only Jehovah, the true God of the Bible, deserves our reverence. Why?

Out of all the beings in this universe, only Jehovah God has intrinsic worth. Intrinsic means, "belonging to the essence of a thing" or "inherent." In other words, only God has value totally in and of Himself. All else derives its value from its association with Him.

In Christian thought, man, made in the image of God, is recognized as having tremendous value. Because of that value, we strive to treat one another with dignity and respect. We love one another, communicate with one another, marry one another, and even legislate laws to protect one another. But in the final analysis, we still must recognize that our dignity is a *derived* dignity. We value one another because God has placed a value on us. Only God derives His value from no other source.

God also deserves our worship because He alone is the Creator. Only He had the power to call forth the creative energies that filled our world with life. When Job—the Old Testament patriarch who lost his family, wealth, and health—began to yield to the influence of ungodly friends and started to lose his confidence in God, the Lord reminded Job of His role as Creator:

Where were you when I laid the foundation of the earth? Tell Me, if you have understanding, who set its measurements? . . . Or who stretched the line on it? On what were its bases sunk? Or who laid its cornerstone? . . . Have you ever in your life commanded the morning, and caused the dawn to know its place? . . . Have you entered into the springs of the sea? Or have you walked in the recesses of the deep? . . . Can you lead forth a constellation in its season? . . . Can you send forth lightnings that they may go and say to you, "Here we are"? Can you draw out Leviathan with a fishhook? . . . Will the faultfinder contend with the Almighty? (Job 38:4-6, 12, 16, 32, 35; 41:1; 40:2)

As God says, *He is the Creator.* Who are we to question His existence, His power, or His sovereignty?

We worship God, then, because of His intrinsic worthship, His creative power, and His redeeming works. In God's prelude to the Law, He identified Himself with these words: "I am the Lord your God, who brought you out of the land of Egypt, out of the house of slavery" (Ex. 20:2).

Before He gave His Laws, He wanted to remind the people who He was. "Just a short time ago, you were slaves. You were oppressed. You were humiliated and beaten and deprived. So I sent Moses to lead you to freedom. Then I sent the plagues to assure your release. Then I parted the Red Sea. Then I drowned the Egyptian host. Yes, it was I who delivered you.

"Then I sustained you in the desert. I led you with a fiery cloud when you needed direction. I provided manna and quail when you were hungry. I caused water to flow from the rock when you were thirsty.

"Did Baal do that for you? Did the foreign god, Moleck, do that for you? Did *any* other gods do that for you? *Could* they have done it for you? No! I alone had the power to create you, and I alone have the power to sustain you against that which would destroy you. Why would you waste your time worshiping another god?"

11

Anyone who has ever seen the pathetic sight of human beings bowing down before idols knows why God gave this command in such absolute terms. I once visited a missionary friend in the South American nation of Paraguay. In a little tribal village not far from the capital city of Asuncion, we watched as diseased, poverty-stricken villagers fell down on their knees and paid homage to a statue made of chiseled stone. The hopelessness of that scene was indelibly printed in my mind.

I wanted to shout, "Don't waste your worship on that stone! What has that stone done for you? What will it *ever* do for you?"

The One who deserves our worship is the intrinsically worthy God. He has the creative power to bring us into being, and the sustaining power to redeem us from despair.

A Living God

When we recognize God's intrinsic worth, we realize how important it is to worship Him, and Him alone. But as I mentioned before, it is not simply for *His honor* that He demands our worship. He also requires it for *our good*. He knows that no other being can satisfy the needs and yearnings of our hearts.

Bowing down before any god but the true and living God of Scripture is like hugging a mannequin. It can't respond. It can't produce. It can't offer anything to anyone.

Psalm 115 notes the sovereignty and power of Israel's God, then contrasts His character with the impotence of foreign gods.

> Their idols are silver and gold, the work of man's hands. They have mouths, but they cannot speak; they have eyes, but they cannot see; they have ears, but they cannot hear; they have noses, but they cannot smell; they have hands, but they cannot feel; they have feet, but they cannot walk; they cannot make a sound with their throat (Ps. 115:4-7).

In modern-day language, the psalmist is saying, "Don't be a fool. At some time in your life you're going to have needs. You're going to have trouble, or crisis, or tragedy—and if you call out to the wrong god, you're not going to get an answer. You're not going to get any help."

During times of grief or disappointment, when it's easy to slip into doubt and confusion, we need a God who can speak to us. We need a God who can give us a word of truth or encouragement or challenge or chastisement. That's the kind of God Jehovah is. He can speak to us through His Word, the Bible, or through the inner witness of the Holy Spirit, who indwells every believer. As unbelievable as it may seem, the true God has the power to speak miraculously to His children right at the point of their greatest need.

The true God also has eyes that see us. He can watch over and protect us. And He has ears that hear us. When we pour out our hearts to Him, we are not engaging in a futile exercise. God hears and He understands. Because of that truth, the psalmist can encourage us to "pour out our hearts before Him" (62:8).

God even has a nose that can smell; that is, He can "sniff out" evil. If sin is making the aroma of our lives unpleasant, God can detect that, and He can convict us and challenge us to greater conformity to His will. I need that. And if you're honest with yourself, you'll admit that you need it too. Without constant accountability to an all-knowing Being who cannot be fooled, we might easily yield to the temptation to live lives of unchecked deception.

We need too a God with hands that can touch us. Though we know God is a spirit, figurative language can help us understand aspects of His Being which are best understood in human terms. To say that God has hands tells us that He can respond to us personally, engulf us with His presence, "touch" us.

To say that God has feet tells us that He is dynamic, not static. He is active. He moves. He can accompany us. As the old Sunday School song said, "Wherever you go, whatever you do, He'll be there."

13

In short, Psalm 115 tells us that the true God of Scripture is a living, responsive, dynamic, creative, thinking, feeling, hearing, touching, moving, loving God—the kind of God we want and need—and the only God worthy of our worship.

The Object of Our Affections

If you're an open-minded person who is devoted to spiritual truth, you've undoubtedly been able to understand and affirm every truth I've stated thus far. You may even have wondered why I've bothered to say it. Am I afraid you're worshiping strange deities? Do I suspect you're bowing down to foreign idols?

In one sense, such thoughts are the farthest things from my mind. I highly doubt that anyone reading this book is involved in the conscious, deliberate worship of gods other than the true God.

In another sense, however, I fear that many well-intentioned Christians have carelessly permitted a multitude of other concerns to become their "gods." They've allowed these concerns to usurp the position of prominence that Jehovah God should have in their affections.

Are you *really* worshiping the true and living God? Does He have ultimate authority in your life? Is He the chairman of the board? The chief executive officer?

To help you answer those questions honestly, let me ask you another question about your affections. Of whom, or what, do you find yourself thinking during quiet moments of free time?

I realize that most people, including myself, do not have a lot of free thought time. Our thoughts usually are directed toward specific tasks, responsibilities, or conversations— whether we're at home, school, or in the marketplace. But at isolated moments—while we're jogging, driving, waiting in lines, or lying down at night—our minds do have the freedom to focus on whatever we choose.

At such times, where does your mind go? To whom or what

do your thoughts automatically turn when they're free to roam?

Several years ago, my brother bought his son, Cameron, a compass for Christmas. Cam was so thrilled with his gift that he could barely control his excitement.

"Hey, Uncle Bill, look what I got from Dad!" he said. "It's a compass. I can shake it up and turn it all around. But when I hold it still again, it always points north. The needle spins around a few times, but in the end, it always goes north!"

Our minds, like the needle in that compass, can focus on a variety of subjects throughout the day. But in the end, when they're left alone to settle, they'll focus on the objects of our greatest affection.

Where does your mind settle? On your job? On your girlfriend or boyfriend? On athletic pursuits? On your dream house? On money? On potential accomplishments? On recreation or pleasure?

Please spend a moment contemplating these questions. Your answers probably will reveal the real gods in your life. The person who truly has "no other gods" before the living God, usually will find that his thoughts "swing around" until they focus on God. He thinks about God. He meditates on the truths he knows about God. He prays to God. He worships God. Jehovah really is the object of his greatest affection.

Is that experience true for you and me? Do our thoughts prove that it is?

Whom Are We Trying to Impress?

Year after year after year, we pour our time, energies, and ambitions into a multitude of demanding activities. We study, we work, we save, we buy, we push ourselves, we achieve. And for what? Why do we do it? Whom are we trying to impress? This is another question that can help us determine the real god in our lives.

Some people say they're simply out to impress themselves. They want to do what pleases and satisfies themselves: they really don't care what anybody else thinks — including God. They're concerned about *their* desires, *their* goals, *their* values. For all practical purposes, they worship themselves. They have become their own god.

Other individuals admit they're basically people-pleasers. They want to impress the guys at the country club, the neighbors next door, the people at work, or their friends at school. And they'll do *anything* to accomplish that goal. They have, in effect, allowed other people's opinions to become their god.

People who obey and apply the first commandment, however, learn to be God-pleasers. They are aware of their desires and personal ambitions, but aren't controlled by them. They have close friendships, but they don't allow other people's opinions to dictate their behavior. They want only to impress God.

These people regularly find themselves on their knees, saying, "O God, today I want to be Yours. I want to live according to Your Word. I want Your Spirit to lead me. I want to be obedient. And I don't care what it costs."

Is that prayer our prayer? Or do we bail out if pleasing God costs us a little pleasure? Or if it costs us men's applause? Whom are we really trying to impress?

What Are We Living For?

A third question that will help us determine our true god involves our life's objectives. We have only one life to live; then we will be called to give an account of what we did with it. When that time comes, what will we have to look back on? What will have been our major objective in life?

Will it have been pleasure? Or the building of an empire? Or the gaining of a position? Or the wielding of power? Will it simply have been to be a "nice guy"?

We have to ask ourselves these questions. What are we trying to accomplish? For what are we living?

The person who understands and obeys the first commandment claims the discovery of God's will as his ultimate objective in life. And he wants not only to discover it, but to pursue it with a passion. He willingly bows before God and implores the Lord to give him a mission in life.

"Show me Your will," he prays, "and I'll gladly do it. If I can serve You best in the business world, then that's where I'll go. If You want me to go to school, then that's what I'll do. If You want me at home, I'll stay there. If You want me in the ministry, I'll accept that responsibility. Give me a mission and I'll pursue it with passion for the rest of my life!"

Is that our major objective in life? Or have we let competing gods lure us from that goal?

Are You Willing?

If God really is on the throne of your life, your thoughts automatically will turn in His direction, your desire will be to impress Him, and your ultimate objective in life will be to determine His will and do it. If those things are not true in your life, then you're kidding yourself. You're worshiping a false god.

In January 1983, a close friend from my church allowed my wife and me to vacation in his condominium near Palm Springs, California. I started each day of our vacation by jogging through the desert around the condominium complex. The morning air was cool and comfortable and the rising sun softly illuminated the purple mountains in the distance. After running for fifteen or twenty minutes the first morning, the panorama of the surrounding beauty compelled me to kneel in the sand and worship God.

Each morning I returned to that same spot to meditate on all God had done for me and to evaluate my commitment to Him. By the end of the week, I knew I had to renew and verbalize my allegiance to the Lord.

"O God," I prayed, "1982 has come and gone, and now I face a new year. This year I want to worship You and set my affections on You more than I ever did before. I want to strive to please You alone. And I want to pursue the ministry You have given me with heightened passion. I want You to be the God of my life — the ultimate authority."

Can you tell God that? Can you tell Him that He's the only one worthy of your worship, that He's the object of your greatest affection? Can you honestly say that He is the only One you want to please? Do you sincerely desire to know His will so you can pursue it?

The Ten Commandments were not arranged in a haphazard, random order. The first commandment is given its place of prominence for a good reason. All our efforts to please and obey God must begin at this point. Unless we're willing to acknowledge — and then deny — our allegiance to the false gods we've created, we'll be unable to make progress along the path of obedience.

Before you leave this chapter, examine your heart and your mind. What is the object of your greatest affection? Who are you trying to impress? What is your major objective?

Does the true God really have first place in your life?

Two
Don't Settle for Shadows

"You shall not make for yourself an idol, or any likeness of what is in heaven above or on the earth beneath or in the water under the earth. You shall not worship them or serve them; for I, the Lord your God, am a jealous God, visiting the iniquity of the fathers on the children, on the third and the fourth generations of those who hate Me, but showing loving-kindness to thousands, to those who love Me and keep My commandments" (Exodus 20:4-6).

I hope that as you read the previous chapter, you were challenged to search the deepest recesses of your inner life. I hope that you were motivated to expose and denounce any false gods you found lurking there. If you did, then I know you're experiencing a greater sense of liberation and joy than you've ever felt before. You're undoubtedly excited about the prospect of living a life more completely in tune with the will of God.

I suspect you're also confident, in regard to the second commandment, that you'll be found perfectly blameless. After all, you've never been one to fashion heathen idols. And you're certainly not going to start doing it now, having just renewed your personal commitment to the Lord.

But if you're like me, you might just find that this second commandment sneaks up on you rather unsuspectingly, touching you with the power of its subtle truth.

A Natural Progression

Let's assume that you've truly placed God on the throne of your life, and He is responding to your obedience — just as He promised in His Word. He is liberating you from the oppressive bonds of sin. He is blessing you with inner contentment and peace. He is giving you hope for the future and a worthy goal to live for. What happens to a person who is on the receiving end of such blessings?

Essentially, he becomes motivated to worship and obey God *even more*. And as he does so, he gets caught up in an ongoing cycle of blessing and worship. The more he honors God with his obedience and worship, the more God blesses him. That increased blessing prompts in him an even greater desire to obey and worship. The cycle goes round and round until the overwhelmed believer joins the psalmist and asks, "What shall I render to the Lord for all His benefits toward me?" (116:12)

Now the sincere believer must ask Himself some questions. Since I have given Him my life, my obedience, my worship, my time, my talents, and my treasures, what more can I do? How can I show Him my appreciation and my adoration?

As the Christian ponders these questions, a new yearning — both exciting and dangerous — begins to grow in his heart. His inner worship begins to plead for an outward expression. He wants to verbalize his love for God and he finds himself singing songs of worship and praise — and enjoying it tremendously! He finds himself praying with greater freedom, intensity, and frequency. He even begins to bow down on his knees as an expression of humility and submission. He wants to show in a tangible way the intangible worship that is welling up in his heart.

His reactions toward God are similar to ones I've experienced toward my kids. There have been times when I'm sitting in the family room reading the newspaper and watching the kids play, that I've been overwhelmed with love for them. At such times, I just have to throw the paper aside and grab one of them. "Oh no, it's a *love attack!*" my daughter happily screams as I pour out my affection in a big bear hug.

Genuine love calls out for expression; and as the intensity of that love grows, the desire to express it in increasingly tangible forms also grows. So it is that over the course of history, believers who were filled with love for God began to feel that desire to give tangible form to their worship. They wanted to facilitate and enhance their devotion by focusing on objects that would attract their attention and call them to worship.

That desire seems innocent enough, doesn't it? On the surface it seems harmless, even commendable. And yet, in the face of that natural and overwhelming desire, God says, "No graven images. No likeness of anything that is in heaven above, earth beneath, or in the water under the earth. No worship helpers."

Why is this? Is God being unreasonable? Does He question our motives? What was going through His mind when He gave that commandment?

I think the answer is obvious. No image constructed by human hands could ever accurately represent the totality, the transcendency, and the majesty of God. We could never shape, paint, or chisel anything that would be an adequate representation of who God is. To attempt to do so would be like asking a scholar to explain the history of the world in one sentence, or a sculptor to make a replica of Mount Rushmore on a single grain of sand, or a musician to play Beethoven's Fifth Symphony with a referee's whistle. It just can't be done. It's absurd even to suggest it!

God knows that any image we might use to portray Him would depict Him as less than He truly is. It would reduce His power, His character, and His mysterious holiness. Eventually, we probably would begin to conceive of Him in ways that mirrored the image we constructed, rather than as the mighty God of Scripture. We would end up worshiping not Him, but merely a shadow of who He really is. And He doesn't want us to dishonor Him or waste our time by worshiping a shadow.

More Than a Golden Calf

It's a tragic irony that while God was giving Moses this commandment, the nation of Israel was engaged in the very activity which it forbids. Exodus tells us that during Moses' extended stay on the mountain, the people began to doubt he would ever return to lead them. As a result, they decided to "make a god" that could go on before them. Aaron, their leader during Moses' absence, gathered together gold jewelry from the people, melted it down, and fashioned it into a golden bull. Then he built an altar before it and said, "Tomorrow shall be a feast to the Lord" (32:5).

While some commentators believe that in building their golden calf, the Israelites abandoned the true God, others believe they had no such intention. Aaron's declaration of a feast "to the Lord" seems to indicate that he, at least, had not turned to another god. He was simply yielding to the people's request for a tangible image of their God. As one commentator has noted: "They required, like children, to have something to strike their senses . . . some visible material object as the symbol of the Divine presence, which should go before them" (Robert Jamieson, *Critical and Experimental Commentary*, vol. 1, Eerdmans, p. 405). In other words, if the Israelites couldn't have their visible, human leader, Moses, at least they would have a portrayal of a God which they could see, touch, and display.

In their fear, they incorporated pagan religious practices into their worship. They probably formed the bull in imitation of a popular Egyptian ceremony that did "homage to the creative power and energy of nature, through the sensuous representation of a three years' old ox" (Jamieson, p. 407). Perhaps Aaron felt that the bull, the paragon of power and potency, was an appropriate symbol for the true God. After all, hadn't God just done some pretty powerful things? He had sent the plagues, He had parted the Red Sea, He had provided manna and quail and water. Certainly, reasoned the Israelites, God would not be offended if they portrayed Him as a strong and powerful bull!

But God *was* offended. So offended, in fact, that only Moses' impassioned plea for mercy kept the Lord from destroying the nation altogether.

Why was He so intensely angered? Because He knew that a bull—or any other tangible symbol—could portray only a miniscule portion of His true character. Yes, the bull portrayed His power; but what of His holiness, His majesty, His love?

Less than twenty-four hours after making the golden calf, the Israelites' worship had degenerated into a sacrilegious orgy. Could it be that they focused their attention on God's power, and forgot about His holiness? Could it be that their imitation of Egyptian ceremony blinded their eyes to the mystery of God's absolute moral perfection?

The Israelites "meant the calf to be an image—a visible sign or symbol of Jehovah, so that their sin consisted not in a breach of the *first* but of the *second* commandment" (Jamieson, p. 407). In other words, they didn't turn to a false god; they merely made an image of the real God. But that image proved to be their downfall! Why? Because like all images, it was unable to portray the fullness of God's identity. As a result, it hindered rather than helped their worship; it led them down the crooked path of disobedience.

An Innocent Rebellion

The blatant sin of the Israelites is obvious. But what do their story and the second commandment have to do with contemporary Christians who clearly know better than to create a golden calf?

To answer that question, I'm going to have to "tiptoe through a mine field." I realize I'll probably detonate a few bombs and catch a little shrapnel along the way; but this journey must be made if I am to be sensitive to the implications of God's commandment.

In my opinion, some modern-day images and objects ought to be evaluated carefully in the light of this commandment. For example, many people, particularly those brought up in the Roman Catholic tradition, give the crucifix an honored place in the vast array of religious symbols. Picturing Jesus on the cross, in pain and agony dying for the sins of the world, the crucifix is a graphic portrayal of the greatest act of love ever demonstrated on this planet. It reminds us of a real event that is precious to all true believers. What could possibly be wrong with praying in the presence of a crucifix or attaching value to it?

The problem, says J.I. Packer, is that the crucifix highlights Jesus' human weakness without conveying His divine strength. It depicts the reality of His pain and suffering, but fails to remind us of His victory and joy. It shows us a dying Jesus, but neglects to show us a living Jesus bursting forth from the tomb with resurrection power (*Knowing God,* InterVarsity Press, pp. 40–41).

I have no problem with what the crucifix depicts, only with what it *fails* to depict. It fails to give us an accurate picture of the totality of who our God is. It conveys only a fraction of His true identity.

Perhaps many of you are thinking, "Come on, give it a break. An image can't convey *everything*." That's exactly my point! Images *can't* convey everything. So God says, "Don't try. Don't use them. They can't do the job!"

We've had an ongoing discussion at our church for years concerning the Protestant version of the crucifix, the empty cross. Some have questioned the integrity of our church because we don't have a large cross prominently displayed in our sanctuary. Some very angry people have accused us of being a cult, of being satanic, or of being liberal in our doctrine. We maintain, however, that while the cross represents the cornerstone of the Christian faith—that Jesus died on the cross to procure our salvation—it's still not the *whole* story.

Why should we hang a cross and not portray the empty tomb? The Apostle Paul said with great conviction that if Jesus Christ did not rise from the dead, then our faith is in vain and we Christians are to be most pitied. We've all been deceived (1 Cor. 15:12-19). Paul certainly would agree that the cross is important, but he would add that the empty grave is every bit as important. So why a cross and not an empty tomb?

Or why an empty tomb and not a manger? The miracle of Jesus' incarnation is as central to our faith as is His death or resurrection. The fact that Jesus, being totally God, also became totally man, is the truth from which our faith derives its significance.

Concern should also be noted in regard to pictures of Jesus. Have you noticed how portraits of Christ have changed over the years? During the 1950s when I was a child, most pictures portrayed Jesus as meek and mild, a pale faced, delicate-looking man who always had a mysterious glow encircling his head. The Jesus of the '60s looked like a campus radical, a fitting leader for a revolutionary age. In the '70s we had a macho Jesus, perfectly proportioned and well-groomed, the obvious creation of a narcissistic society. How will we picture Him in the '80s? Will we squeeze Him into the mold of the young, upwardly mobile middle class? What image of Jesus will please us most and make Him easily acceptable?

Which single emblem can accurately portray the totality of who God is or what Jesus Christ has done for us? Can *you* choose?

A *Shadow* or the *Real Thing?*

The church is called to give people more than a creed, a ceremony, a tradition, a formula, or a shadow. The body of Christ has the matchless privilege and awesome responsibility of giving people what they yearn for in their hearts — truth that will lead them to a daily, dynamic, life-changing relationship with a living Savior. People need to understand that if they repent of

their sins and follow Jesus Christ, they will have a vital relationship with a living God they can worship anywhere, anytime.
They can worship Him in school, at home, in the car, at the
store, in the shower—anywhere! They don't need candles or
altars or statues or crosses or pictures or any other "props"
that might divert their attention from the reality of the true
God.

Scripture tells us that we should worship God in spirit and in
truth (John 4:24). To worship God in spirit means that our
worship involves more than just going through the external
motions of a prescribed form or ritual. True worship involves
our emotions and our will. It involves personal and heartfelt
adoration and submission. To worship God in truth means that
we worship Him intelligently. We worship the God who really
exists, rather than a figment of our imagination. We worship
the God who is revealed to us, not in the one-dimensional
portrayals of religious relics, statues, and pictures, but in the
multifaceted light of His divine character.

Where can we catch a glimpse of that divine character? In the
Bible. God has revealed Himself in His Word. That's why it's so
important that we devote ourselves to sound teaching and diligent personal Bible study. There's no other way to develop an
accurate understanding of who God is. People who ignore the
written, revealed truth about God inevitably end up with a
distorted view of Him.

Many people, unfortunately, perceive God as a tightfisted
judge. They genuinely believe that if they take one step out of
line, they are destined for hell. Even though they have sincerely
put their faith in Jesus Christ, they still live with the proverbial
sword of Damocles hanging over their heads. One false move
will signal their destruction.

I've counseled many people with such a view of God and I've
repeatedly referred them to Psalm 103:8: "The Lord is compas-
sionate and gracious, slow to anger and abounding in loving-
kindness." Yes, God will get angry if we push Him far enough,
if we consciously rebel against Him. But He doesn't get angry
easily. He knows our human frailty and weakness, and His

deepest desire is to show us an abundant measure of His grace and compassion.

Jesus Himself said that He didn't come to condemn the world, but to save it (John 3:17). In saying that, He gave us a crystal clear view of the heart of God. God is no anxious ogre, impatiently waiting for a reason to punish us. He will, indeed, become angry when we force Him to. But His first choice is to win us by His love.

Some people see God as a military general, coldly barking out orders and issuing ultimatums. They have created a God who fits in well with their aggressive, competitive personalities; but they have forgotten that the God of Scripture encourages His children to call Him "Abba, Father," which means "Daddy" (Rom. 8:15-16). Yes, our God is holy and majestic, but He is no military commander to whom we must snap a salute. He is a warm and personal God who invites us to crawl up on His lap and bask in His fatherly love.

Others view God as the actor George Burns portrayed Him in the movies—a funny old man in tennis shoes and glasses. God is their buddy, a nice guy to have around. I get very unnerved by such cocky familiarity with God. It's one thing to enjoy a warm relationship with a personal God, a Heavenly Father. It's quite another to turn that revered Father into a good-time buddy who can share a cold beer and a slap on the back.

Not long ago on a flight to California I sat next to a girl who told me she was living with her boyfriend, had a drinking problem, and frequently used cocaine. Throughout the course of our three-hour conversation, she made casual references to other aspects of her lifestyle that were both illegal and immoral. Finally, the conversation turned to Christianity.

"How do you square your lifestyle with God's will, His wisdom, and His Word?" I asked her.

Without giving it a second thought, she responded with the words all true Christians have grown to know and hate. "Well, *my God* is the grandfatherly type, who loves me and takes care of me and tells me I'm OK. He knows that boys will be boys and girls will be girls. He doesn't care much what I do."

27

It's so much easier for us to *change* God than it is to *conform* to His will. Who wants to face the expectations of a Holy God when they can create a metaphysical grandfather who will pat them benignly on the head and ignore their sin? Who wants an accurate image of a sovereign God when they can create a convenient image that never interferes with their selfish desires?

Someone once wrote that if Julius Caesar or Napoleon entered a filled auditorium, the entire audience would rise and applaud. But if Jesus Christ entered, every man, woman, and child would bow down to the ground and worship Him. The person who wrote that obviously knew, as did the Prophet Isaiah, that the real God of Scripture is more than a pal. When Isaiah experienced his life-changing vision of the Almighty he didn't quip, "Hey, God, nice to see You. I've been looking forward to this for a long time. You're a real sport." Instead, he said, in effect, "Woe is me, for I am a sinful man. How can I survive in the presence of a holy God?" (Isa. 6:5)

Those who see God as a benevolent grandfather or a good ole boy have completely ignored the holiness of God. They have so cheapened His loving-kindness that it has become nothing more than a cosmic joke. Those who see Him as a harsh judge or a military commander have ignored His infinite love and transformed His perfect righteousness into a flaming sword of condemnation. In both cases, they have created images of God that are distorted and inaccurate. J.I. Packer argues that such erroneous mental images are as loathsome to God as was the Israelites' golden bull. The second commandment prohibits them as clearly as any material image created by human hands.

Down with Tyranny!

I recently received a phone call from a man who said he had visited our church and was very troubled because I preached from a plexiglass pulpit. For my benefit, he explained the tradition behind the wooden pulpit, and wondered how I possibly

DON'T SETTLE FOR SHADOWS

could justify deviating from that accepted form. After a lengthy conversation, we cordially agreed to disagree. Still, I was saddened by the fact that we spent half an hour discussing pulpit construction without even once discussing what I proclaimed from it.

How typical that is of the human mind. We focus on wood and plexiglass when we should be focusing on the spiritual truths so compellingly revealed in God's Word. We place undue importance on shadows and neglect the substance of the Christian faith.

How I pray that the church of the twentieth century will be freed from the tyranny of dusty relics that can never represent the totality of our matchless God. May we learn to worship God in spirit and in truth. May we refuse to settle for convenient images, and instead, pursue with diligence a greater knowledge of the one true God.

Will you commit yourself to doing that?

Three
Turn Profanity into Praise

"You shall not take the name of the Lord your God in vain, for the Lord will not leave him unpunished who takes His name in vain" (Exodus 20:7).

Before we delve into the meat of this chapter, I would like you to humor me by taking a little test. It's called the Eavesdropping Accuracy Test. Pretend you're in a restaurant or on a plane, quietly minding your own business; suddenly, the person in the booth or the seat behind you says something you just can't help but overhear. As you mull over the brief bit of conversation you've overheard, you think, *Ah, I know what that person does for a living. I can tell simply by what he said.*

Now that you have, figuratively speaking, entered into that scenario, read the following eight conversation fragments and see if you can determine the occupation of the speakers:

(1) "Spec buying has pretty much squeezed the shorts out of the action."
(2) "Interfaces to service modules as data base handlers can be packaged using macros."
(3) "We had to cantilever those joists."

(4) "Fifty percent of the line is a facultative placement and the other 50 percent is on a treaty with an excess loss provision at $1 million."

(5) "She's going to require an equilibration before we can do any final restoration."

(6) "I ordered a CBC right away."

(7) "The kerygmatic imperative is teleologically soteriological."

(8) "The apgar score was ten."

Now that you've scribbled your answers in the upper margin of this page, let's see how perceptive an eavesdropper you are. The correct answers are:

(1) A stockbroker or commodities trader
(2) A computer programmer
(3) A carpenter
(4) An insurance salesman
(5) A dentist
(6) A doctor (ordering a Complete Blood Count)
(7) A Bible professor
(8) A pediatrician or delivery room nurse

Were you able to guess all eight professions correctly? If not, don't feel bad. Few people do. If, however, you work in any of those occupations, or if you are closely associated with someone who does, I'm sure you guessed those particular professions correctly. Certain phrases and words are dead give aways. Whenever you hear them, you can come to some fairly accurate conclusions about the person who used them.

In this chapter, I want to discuss some other words and phrases that are clear tip-offs. They don't tell us about the occupations of the speakers, but they do indicate something very important about the inner lives of the people who use them.

Obviously, I'm talking about the words and phrases forbidden in the third commandment. When we hear someone use the names of God or Jesus Christ as obscenities—or as convenient expressions of anger, frustration, or fear—we know im-

mediately that they have not yet had a real glimpse of the
majesty, holiness, and wonder of God.

More Than Just a Word

The first commandment tells us we need to have the right God
on the throne of our lives. The second commandment counsels
us to make sure we really are worshiping *Him,* and not just a
shadow of who He is. The third commandment now tells us
that even His name is to be held in honor and respect. Every
time we utter God's name, or sing it, we must do so thoughtfully. We should never use His name frivolously or mechanically,
and it goes without saying that we should never use it
profanely.

Why do you think God gave this commandment the number
three spot on His top ten list of eternal do's and don'ts? Why is
His name so important? Quite simply, every time we say the
name of God, we think about the Being behind that name. And
even if that thought lasts no longer than a fraction of a second,
it is a thought that either honors or dishonors God.

Tim Vandenbos, the director of our church camp, used to
have a German shepherd named Jesse, which he bought while
serving in the Army overseas. Stationed in a guard tower for
long stretches of time without human companionship, Tim developed a warm relationship with his dog. Naturally, the dog
developed an intense loyalty to Tim.

Years later, at our camp in upper Michigan, Jesse still followed Tim everywhere. They separated only when Tim had to go
down the river for supplies. Then Jesse would lay on the dock,
ears drooping and sick at heart, to await Tim's return. Some of
the camp workers who knew of Tim's relationship with his dog
occasionally walked down to the beach to have a little fun.

"Hey, Jesse," they would taunt, "where's Ralph?" Jesse
would not respond.

"Hey, Jesse," they would try again, "where's Joe?" Still no
response.

"Hey, Jesse, where's *Tim?*" At that point, Jesse would go wild! His ears would perk up, his tail would wag, and he'd start running back and forth along the beach, hoping to hear the sound of Tim's returning boat.

Even a dog is able to have thoughts about his master. The mere mention of Tim's name awakened Jesse's feelings of affection for him. A single word brought his master to mind.

So it is when we hear, speak, or sing the name of God. Immediately, the truths we know about the One behind that name come into our minds. The third commandment tells us that when such thoughts occur, we'd better be prepared to worship—for the Being who comes to mind is the intrinsically worthy God who created and sustains us, and who gives us hope for the future.

Does It Really Matter to God?

We read in Leviticus that the son of an Israelite woman got into a scuffle with another man. During the course of the fight, the Israelite "blasphemed the Name and cursed" (24:11). In ancient Israel, there was no doubt as to which "Name" was so revered that its use as a curse constituted blasphemy. Only one name was so honored. The name of God.

In my mind I can envision the scene. The Israelite man has his dukes up—ready to fight—but he misses the chance to deflect a punch, and the other guy hits him square on the chin. In frustration and anger he curses, using the very name of God.

Unfortunately for him, some men who knew the commandments of God heard his blasphemous curse. After the fight they took him before Moses and asked Moses what should be done with someone who cursed *The Name*. Moses communicated God's answer: "Stone him." God's judgment was death.

In effect, God was saying, "What right does a sinner have to shake his little fist in anger and blaspheme the name of the Holy God? That is the height of audacity. It just can't be tolerated!"

"But," you may say, "that was during Old Testament times. Things have changed since then. What does the New Testament say?"

As a matter of fact, Jesus *did* have something very important to say about God's name. But before we look at that, join me, if you will, in another little exercise in creative thinking.

Imagine that you are one of the charter members of my church. Since the beginning of our church ministry you have faithfully attended services and have willingly used your spiritual gifts to serve the Lord and others. On top of that, you and I have developed a close personal friendship and have been very involved in the joys and sorrows of each others' lives over the years.

Now, let's suppose that one Sunday I stood up in front of the congregation and said, "Friends, I think this will be one of the most important messages I'll ever give. Certainly it is one that will touch on the subjects closest to my heart. This morning, I want to share with you the top five prayer concerns of my life. I hope you'll join me in making these concerns your top priorities too."

If you heard me say those words and sensed I was speaking from the depths of my heart, what would you, my fellow worker in the kingdom and personal friend, do? How would you respond? I suspect you'd take out a piece of paper, write down my five concerns, and make them a regular part of your personal prayer life.

Now let's imagine that it was not I, but Jesus Himself, who stood before you in the flesh. And let's suppose *He* wanted to share *His* most important prayer concerns with you. Do you have any doubts about how you'd respond to His quietly spoken, "Please listen carefully"? Of course not! You, and every true believer in that sanctuary, would grab a pencil and paper as fast as you could and wait in eager anticipation. The very Son of God, the Savior, was going to share the greatest concerns of His heart with you. What an honor! What a privilege!

That imaginary situation closely mirrors the circumstances surrounding Jesus' teaching of the Lord's Prayer. When Jesus' disciples asked Him how to pray, He responded by giving them an adaptable pattern for prayer–and a glimpse into His own prayer life.

"Our Father who art in heaven," He began, "hallowed be Thy name" (Matt. 6:9). After clearly establishing the identity of the One to whom He prayed, He immediately expressed His number one concern—that God's name be hallowed. He wanted it to be reverenced and honored and used only in a way that would bring God glory.

Can we doubt Jesus' feelings on this subject? Can we doubt God's seriousness about how we use His name? Certainly not. Yet this is probably one of the most frequently broken commandments of all. We'd do well to understand why that is.

The Uninformed

It's safe to say that people who dishonor the name of God can be placed in one of three categories. The first category includes those individuals who misuse God's name out of ignorance. They are uninformed, completely oblivious to what the Lord has revealed in His Word concerning the use of His name. Perhaps they are unchurched and have not had any teaching on this subject. Perhaps they've never read the Bible for themselves. Whatever the reason, they're not aware of the seriousness of what they're doing.

Because of an experience I had as a boy, I have no trouble relating to this type of uninformed behavior. My father ran a wholesale produce company that his father had founded, and which my brother now runs. When I was in second grade my father started taking me to the warehouse on Saturday mornings, where I worked with the dockworkers and truck drivers.

Needless to say, that was a rather rough group of people for a second-grader to be rubbing shoulders with on a regular basis. And along the way, I learned a few things I probably shouldn't have—including a few four-letter words. Unfortunately, the dockworkers used these words constantly and in such a casual manner that I didn't realize anything was wrong with them. In fact, I thought they were quite versatile words one could use to express any emotion from surprise to frustration to outright anger.

One Saturday afternoon, after returning from the warehouse, I was in my bedroom with my older brother, Dan. Regrettably, Dan thought it was his responsibility to do to me what every big brother does to his younger brother—degrade and humiliate me! I recall he took that responsibility very seriously; he made it clear that he considered me a real loser, a nerd, a wimp. Nothing I did ever impressed him or made him proud of me. Everything I did was minor-league kid's stuff . . . until that particular Saturday afternoon.

As usual, we were in my room, when I accidentally dropped a model I had been building on the floor. In frustration, I blurted out a new word I had learned from the dockhands. Boy, was Dan surprised—and impressed. He stared at me with eyes as big as saucers, and slowly a giant smile spread across his face. I could tell he thought that was just about the neatest thing I had ever said. I went from the minor leagues to the majors.

During the next forty-five minutes I used that word over and over again. And each time Dan smiled as if to say, "You're really something, Billy. You've got guts for a little guy!"

At dinnertime, Mom, Dad, and all five of us kids sat around the big kitchen table the way we always did, a perfect picture of a nice Norman Rockwell family. Near the end of the meal, my dad asked what Dan and I were going to do after dinner. Dan shrugged his shoulders as if he didn't care, but I decided to be a little more expressive. Leaning back in my chair, I jauntily cocked my head to the side. Then I casually said one of my newly acquired words—the way I'd heard the dockhands say it to express an "I don't care" attitude.

I looked at Dan to catch his smile, but for some reason he wasn't smiling. On the contrary, he looked horror-stricken. As my eyes darted around the table, I saw that my older sister was gasping for air, my mother was starting to cry, and my dad was slowly backing out of his chair, coming my way. I knew then that I'd been had.

My dad grabbed me by the shoulders and carried me about six inches off the floor all the way down to my bedroom. I turned around for one last look; my brother was beaming from ear to ear.

All the way down the stairs I begged for mercy. "Dad, I didn't know. Dan tricked me. He thought it was cool. I didn't know. I didn't know. I didn't. . . ."

I honestly didn't know that the word was a problem. In my naiveté I thought anything so commonly used and so obviously impressive had to be all right. I was genuinely ignorant of the truth.

Perhaps some of you have slipped into the careless use of God's name. After all, it's commonly used in school, in the marketplace, in the neighborhood. Perhaps you have been unaware, though, that this is a grievous sin—a sin so serious that in the Old Testament it led to death. In this matter there is no room for ignorance.

If you have dishonored God's name in ignorance, I challenge you right now to implore His forgiveness and commit yourself to obedience. Decide right now that you're never going to profane His name again.

You are no longer ignorant.

The Uncontrolled

Some people profane God's name because they don't know any better; others do so simply because they can't control their tongues. They know the Ten Commandments forbid profanity, and they fully intend to obey them, but sometimes they just lose control. In fits of anger or frustration—when they're cut off in traffic, when they hit their thumb with a hammer, when the baby cries at night—they slip. They lose control and use God's name carelessly.

For these people, profanity is the exception, not the rule. They are crushed when they realize they've dishonored God's name. They know they have sinned and they repent immediately and ask for God's forgiveness.

The Bible openly acknowledges the difficulty of controlling the tongue. Scripture tells us that every species of beast, bird, reptile, and sea animal can be tamed by the human race; but no one can control the human tongue (James 3:7-8). Yet God says that we *must* control it. We must make every effort to use our tongues for honor, not for dishonor. So what do we do? How can we make sure we'll never profane God's name again?

We can begin by examining our hearts. Jesus said, "The good man out of the good treasure of his heart brings forth what is good; and the evil man out of the evil treasure brings forth what is evil; for the mouth speaks from that which fills his heart" (Luke 6:45).

Jesus is saying here that neither good intentions nor self-discipline can keep us from losing control of our tongues if there's sin in our hearts. When the pressure is on, the rebellion—or bitterness, anger, or hatred—that's hidden in the recesses of our inner lives, will erupt into an explosion of profanity. The only sure way to clean up our mouths, then, is to clean up our hearts.

Fortunately, we don't have to clean up our hearts alone; the Holy Spirit will help us. We begin by *asking* for His divine intervention. The Holy Spirit is no tyrant who imposes His work on us against our will. He waits to be invited. So we begin with an invitation. We ask Him to clean the sin out of our hearts, and then fill us with the fruit of His Spirit—love, joy, peace, patience, kindness, goodness, faithfulness, gentleness, and self-control (Gal. 5:22-23).

We can cooperate with the work of the Holy Spirit by diligently obeying the first and second commandments. That involves yielding to God's authority and realizing that He's more than just a convenient image based on human opinions. He's the holy God of Scripture who deserves our humble adoration.

We also can support the work of the Holy Spirit in our lives by reading the Bible, listening to Christian music, and having spiritually oriented conversations with other believers. The more we saturate our minds with the knowledge of God's holiness and majesty, the less likely we'll be to profane His name. We'll gradually find that profanity rarely comes to mind. If it does, the thought of dishonoring God's name will be appalling. We won't even be tempted to do it.

We'll also find that we want to obey another set of biblical imperatives. These tell us not to allow filthiness, silly talk, or coarse jesting to come out of our mouths (Eph. 5:4). It's not enough to refrain from cursing God's name. We also have to quit telling dirty jokes and using crude language. In fact, we should avoid saying anything that doesn't accurately reflect the grace, purity, and love which the Holy Spirit has placed in our hearts.

The goal of our speech is to "speak the truth in love" (Eph. 4:15). That means we should never speak half-truths, or exaggerated truths, but only the absolute truth — about God, ourselves, and others.

Is that your goal? The truth about God is that His name deserves to be honored — always. Will you allow His Spirit to purify your heart so that every word which flows from it will exalt the name of God?

The Unsaved

For the first twelve months after my father died, I couldn't stand to hear undertaker jokes. When somebody said, "Hey, did you hear the one about the funeral director?" I just wanted to say, "Please, stop. I don't want to hear about that. It's not funny to me."

We have a number of recovering alcoholics at our church. They don't enjoy hearing drunk jokes. Drunkenness is a serious problem that has played havoc with their lives. To them, it's nothing to laugh about.

Similarly, those who have been pierced with the knowledge of their sin find no humor in careless talk that profanes the name of the One who has loved and redeemed them. They have come face to face with the fact that someday they are going to stand before a Holy God. When they do, their good works, their money, their power, their talents, and their accomplishments are going to mean nothing. They'll stand before God empty-handed—unless they repent of their sins and ask Jesus Christ to be their Lord.

So they do that. As a result, they begin to feel a deep sense of peace and assurance. They know they've been forgiven and offered the hope of eternal life. This motivates them to love and worship the Lord. Eventually, they find that the name of Jesus has become precious to them, that the name of God has become a word to be revered. The last thing they want to do is profane those names.

In contrast, there are some people who feel no remorse when they flagrantly violate the third commandment. These people are confirmed unbelievers. They have never confessed Jesus Christ as their personal Savior, and have no regard for God. So it doesn't bother them to take God's name in vain; in fact, they rather seem to enjoy it. It's a way to prove they're not afraid of God. It's a flashing neon sign that says, "I'm in charge here. I'm the boss!"

They're like the teenager who smokes in front of his mom and dad for the first time. For months he's been hiding in alleys and other people's cars, smoking on the sly. Then one day he walks into the family room, lights up, takes a long drag, and looks his parents straight in the eyes. In effect, he's announcing, "You don't scare me anymore. You have no control over me. I don't care what you think or how you feel."

Unbelievers who profane God's name are saying essentially the same thing. And some of them have been saying it for thirty, forty, even fifty years. Are you one of those people? Are you someone who flaunts your profanity in the face of God?

If you are, I have bad news and good news for you. The bad news is that someday you're going to come face to face with a righteous God, and you're going to have to account for your filthy mouth. You'll have no excuses, no control, no time to mend your ways. You'll be a deserving victim of the wrath of the God you dishonored for a lifetime.

The good news is, the same God you've been cursing loves

you. Right this minute He's waiting to open His arms and embrace you as His child. All you have to do is repent. Just say, "Lord, I'm the one with the filthy mouth—the one who's been cursing Your name. I'm the one who's been shaking my puny little fist in rebellion. And now I'm sorry. I ask for your forgiveness. I don't want Jesus Christ to be my favorite curse word. I want Him to be my Savior."

The Lord of the universe is head over heels in love with us—the frail, sinful inhabitants of a tiny planet. We don't deserve His love, but He gives it to us anyway. Though we have cursed the name of the One who spilled His blood for us, God still says, "Come. Repent. Be My child."

Doesn't that make you want to offer God a heart that's pure and lips that honor His name? The psalmist said, "O Lord, our Lord, how majestic is Thy name in all the earth!" (8:9) Our occupation throughout eternity will be to worship the Lord and to exalt His name. But why wait? Why not join the psalmist now in declaring the majesty of God's name?

Four
Follow the
Maintenance Schedule

"Remember the Sabbath Day, to keep it holy. Six days you shall labor and do all your work, but the seventh day is a Sabbath of the Lord your God; in it you shall not do any work, you or your son or your daughter, your male or your female servant or your cattle or your sojourner who stays with you. For in six days the Lord made the heavens and the earth, the sea and all that is in them, and rested on the seventh day; therefore the Lord blessed the Sabbath Day and made it holy" (Exodus 20:8-11).

A member of my church owns and drives an airport limousine for a living. As he was taking my wife and me to the airport several weeks ago, I asked him how many miles he thought he would get out of his limo. He told me he had driven his previous vehicle over 400,000 miles without a single major engine repair, and he fully expected to do the same with his current one.

I was dumbfounded. "How can you possibly put that many miles on a car?"

He answered with a single word: "Maintenance."

The importance of proper vehicle maintenance is no secret. Every owner's manual has a section entitled "Maintaining Your

Car," which provides an upkeep schedule designed to assure optimal performance and longevity. Periodically, the oil and air filter should be changed, the tires rotated, the undercarriage lubricated, and various parts routinely replaced. The list goes on and on, and people who want to maintain their cars conscientiously heed such advice.

But maintenance is the key to more than optimal car performance. It's also essential to optimal *human* performance. And if a car needs an owner's manual to define proper maintenance, so do we. Fortunately, we have one—the Bible. One of the many benefits that this owner's manual provides is a "Maintenance Law"—the fourth commandment—which tells us how to maintain a level of peak performance in our lives through a wisely designed upkeep schedule.

There's More to Life Than Labor

God begins the fourth commandment with a positive statement—"Remember the Sabbath Day, to keep it holy"—and clarifies it with a negative statement—"In it you shall not do any work." Then, as if He anticipates our resistance to this simple command, He silences us with a refresher course on the sequence of Creation.

Genesis 1 tells us that on the first day God called forth light, and separated the day from the night. On the second day He created the vast expanse of sky called "the heavens." On the third day He caused the dry land to appear and covered it with vegetation. On the fourth day He created the sun, the moon, and the stars. On the fifth and sixth days He filled the earth with animals. Then, finally, He created man. From the dust of the ground He formed him, and breathed into his nostrils the breath of life.

During six distinct periods of time, God moved from the most basic elements of creation to the most phenomenally complex. *So what now?* we wonder. *What's left for Him to do on the seventh day?*

Genesis tells us that "by the seventh day God completed His work which He had done; and He rested on the seventh day from all His work which He had done. Then God blessed the seventh day and sanctified it, because in it He rested from all His work which God had created and made" (2:2-3).

"Ah ha!" you say. "I get it. God was exhausted. After six straight days of strenuous labor, He needed a break!"

But can that possibly be the point of this passage? Doesn't Scripture tell us repeatedly that God never wearies, never slumbers, never sleeps? Doesn't the Word clearly show us that nothing can exhaust the inexhaustible God?

Of course it does! So obviously, God was not trying to illustrate His personal fatigue. He was, instead, introducing a maintenance plan for the human race. He was so serious about this principle of maintenance, in fact, that He chose to use *Himself* as an example. He wanted to announce to all creation, and all history, that after six days of labor, enough is enough! Labor is a very good thing—but it's not the *only* thing. *There is more to life than labor*.

A Necessary Break

God's intensity in expressing this command borders on the comedic. He simply could have said, "For six days you shall do your work, and on the seventh day you shall rest." That's clear and to the point. But apparently, He wasn't content to make His point so casually.

Instead, the Lord said, essentially, "Let Me make Myself very, very clear. I don't want *you* to work. I don't want *your son* to work. I don't want *your daughter* to work. I don't want *your male servant* or *your female servant* to work. I don't even want *your animals* to work. Give the cattle a break! Take the yoke off the oxen! And if you have *guests* visiting you, don't let them work either. I don't care *who* they are! I want all work to come to a screeching halt!"

God evidently realized that for human beings to function

optimally over the long haul—to maintain an attitude of joy and peace, a positive perspective toward God and other people, and physical and emotional health—they would have to break out of their weekly routines. They would have to get off the treadmill of labor. They would have to set aside one day in seven when they could drop everything and get their minds and bodies back in shape.

Yes, God told us 3,000 years ago what production analysts have concluded only recently: that reasonably spaced and carefully used work breaks clearly increase productivity. Statistics show that after approximately forty hours of work, concentration levels drop, mistakes increase, and morale takes a nose dive. Even one's health is affected. Doctors tell us that workaholics (those seven-day-a-week-workers who mock God's plan) lead the charts in work-related disorders such as high blood pressure and premature heart attacks. If we refuse to cease from our labors on a regular basis, we inevitably will experience the telltale signs of breakdown.

God knew that all along; so He built a work break right into the system—a one day mini-vacation, so to speak—a time for our bodies to recuperate.

But more than our bodies need a break. Our emotions too need a change of pace. In this technologically oriented society, few people experience the physical stress of battered muscles and calloused skin. Many, however, experience the emotional stress that accompanies a schedule filled with too many people and too many demands. They grow weary of phone calls, memos, printouts, appointments, interviews, classes, meetings, forms, credit checks, and deadlines. By 5 P.M. on Friday they're emotional casualties. They start making poor decisions, thus jeopardizing profits. They become short and antagonistic, thus jeopardizing relationships. And everyone around them, in the workplace and at home, can tell they need exactly what God says they need—a break.

Some of you may be thinking, *But I'm a nurse. I'm a pilot. 'm a police officer. Sometimes it's impossible for me to avoid working on Sunday.* I realize that many people in such service

LAWS OF THE HEART

professions occasionally must work on Sunday, and I believe God exhibits grace in regard to such positions of necessity. Still, we should make every effort to avoid working on Sunday. We may have to make some exceptions because of the nature of our work or service, but we should never make these exceptions lightly.

An unusually strong Christian influence permeated the small town in which I grew up. Because of that influence, any place of business that remained open on Sunday was doomed to fail. The Christians in town simply would avoid that restaurant, store, or shopping center. Within six weeks it would be out of business—unless, of course, the proprietor promptly posted a "Closed on Sunday" sign!

The growth of that town, and the accompanying demise of its Christian influence, led to a dramatic revision of the unofficial code of Sabbath Day observance. Today, many local businesses are open on Sunday. For many years, though, the people of that community held to a very important principle. They knew that for one day each week, they had to stop working, and allow themselves to be refreshed physically and cleansed emotionally.

The Flip Side

We know God wants us to *stop working* on the Sabbath. But that's not the whole story. He also wants us to *start worshiping*. That doesn't mean we should neglect worship at other times throughout the week, or that we should halt personal Bible study and prayer. But the Bible tells us that throughout history, God's people have supplemented their personal devotional life by worshiping together on the Sabbath. There *is* more to the Sabbath than the absence of labor. There's also the presence of worship.

The Old Testament Israelites gathered for Sabbath Day worship at the tent of meeting, and later, at the tabernacle. Jesus too went to the local synagogue to worship on the Sabbath, "as was His custom" (Luke 4:16). We also see this pattern of worship continued in the early church. After Jesus' resurrection, the Sabbath was changed from the last day of the week to the first. But the change in day signaled no change in purpose. Early Christians still knew that on the Sabbath they had to stop working and start worshiping.

The author of Hebrews says, in no uncertain terms, that we should not neglect corporate meetings of the church (10:25). Why did God so clearly establish the priority of these weekly gatherings? I think it's because He knew how badly we would need to be chastened, challenged, and changed on a regular basis.

When I stand before my congregation on Sunday mornings, I feel like a doctor performing open-heart surgery. That brief hour and fifteen minutes on Sunday morning is the only time some people open their hearts to the truths of God's Word. For just a little while, they drop the defenses they've hidden behind during the week, and allow God to touch and change their hearts.

The stakes of physical open-heart surgery are weighty—life and death. But those stakes seem inconsequential when we enter the realm of the spiritual. The stakes of spiritual heart surgery are *eternal* life and *eternal* death. Some people wonder why I give my Sunday messages with such passion. It's because I know what the stakes are. How can a minister take the message of eternal destiny lightly? How can *anyone* take it lightly?

We all need to cease from our labors on Sunday and gather together for open-heart surgery. Some people need major surgery. They need to address such crucial issues as sin and death and eternity. Others need minor surgery, repair work. They need a time for confession and challenge. But in one way or another, we all need this time of rest.

We also can benefit from the weekly change that corporate meetings offer. First, we need a physical change. We need to get out of the office, the truck, the school, the plant, the store—out of the place where we perform our labor. We need a new environment, where we can rub shoulders with different people.

We also require an emotional change. We need to hear different language patterns and music. We need to be caught up in a different value system. We need to encounter joy and creativity and meaning.

And, of course, we need a spiritual change. We need to attend a church where God's Word is believed and taught without apology. We need a pastor who doesn't gloss over important issues or trade truth for personal opinions and vain speculations. We need solid, biblical information.

Sometimes on Sunday mornings, when I look out over my congregation, I can sense the work of the Spirit. I can tell that by God's grace, people are being nurtured and challenged. It's tremendously exciting to see that. Yet a nagging question often haunts me. *How long will this spiritual meal last? How long before its nourishing effect wears off?*

I know that in less than twenty-four hours most of these congregants are going back into a secular marketplace, school, or neighborhood. There they'll face a steady stream of heavy challenges. They'll have to compete. They'll have to push and drive themselves. They'll probably get beat up emotionally. And all the while, they'll be bombarded with the destructive messages of the secular media: *Do what you want! Live as you please! Ventilate! Indulge! Win!*

There's a good chance that after three or four days in that type of environment, even the strongest Christian will need another spiritual meal. After six or seven days, there's no question about it. It's high time to replenish the food supply and refocus spiritually.

God knows the inevitable rhythms of our lives. He knows that if we work seven days a week, week after week, we'll begin to lose perspective on the true meaning of life. We'll get to the point where all we care about are bigger barns, more deals, and higher yields. We'll be worn out physically, burned out emotionally, and out of touch with spiritual realities. We'll be caught in a downward spiral that weakens our marriages, our families, our friendships, our health, and even our moral convictions.

But God says, "Hey, I know you and I love you, and I don't want that to happen to you. So quit working! Take a break! Get recharged!"

It's so important for us to attend churches where we can really grow. Recently, a man told me he used to walk to a church two minutes from his home, twice every Sunday, but still was feeling spiritually malnourished. Now he drives forty-five minutes to a different church. There, he's alive, growing, and excited about his faith! For him, a forty-five minute trip was the key to his spiritual life; it took him from a church that didn't meet his spiritual needs to one that did.

What about you? Are you attending a church that recharges you spiritually? Many times I've told members of my congregation that if they're not being fed spiritually at our church, they should go elsewhere. If they don't respect their leaders, if they can't understand the teaching, if there's no place for them to get involved, then they should find a more suitable church.

For three years I've been the chaplain for the Chicago Bears football team. Occasionally, benched players have told me of their frustrations about not playing. They've even shared their fantasies of grabbing the coach and saying, "Hey, if I'm not going to play, just tell me! Let me go to a team where I can play. I want to make a difference. I want to use my skills."

Most of us probably feel just like those football players. We want to contribute. We want to work. We want to be starting members of the team. The good news is that in a properly functioning church, we can be—and *should* be. If that's not true in your church, perhaps you should find a church where there's more of an opportunity to serve.

Someday God is going to say to each of us, "I gave you brains, I gave you resources, and I gave you spiritual abilities. What did you do with them?" If all we can say is that we chose to sit on the bench—dropped in for an hour, put our buck in the basket, and left—we're going to be dreadfully sorry. After all God has done for us, He has the right to expect us to be more than spectators. He has the right to expect us to get off the bench and provide tangible, meaningful service.

But we shouldn't attend church for spiritual growth and service alone. We also should attend a church where we can receive support and encouragement. The biggest problem for "church hoppers" — those who repeatedly move from one church to the next and never call any one place "home" — is that they have to stand alone during times of need. When there's a death in the family or a personal tragedy, they have no one to turn to. For too long they've hopped in and out. Now no one knows them.

Please don't do that. If you're not "part of the family" at a local church, take active steps to change that. Get involved where you are, or find a church where you feel more at home. God commands us to join together, not just to be taught and challenged, but also to be encouraged, refreshed, and surrounded in love. The church is God's gift to us. Don't ever refuse that gift.

Made to Be Enjoyed

Jesus tells us that the Sabbath was created for man's good, and not man for the good of the Sabbath (Mark 2:27). My paraphrase of that verse would read: "Enjoy the Sabbath! That's what it's for. Stop working, start worshiping, and then *enjoy!*"

The church in which I grew up placed a long list of restrictions on Sabbath Day activities. The restrictions undoubtedly stemmed from a sincere desire to honor God, but I don't think these lists of rigid do's and don'ts were what God had in mind when He gave us this commandment. Rather, I believe that our Sabbath Day activities should enhance our physical, emotional, and spiritual recovery in ways that appeal to us personally.

After giving two messages on Sunday morning, I return home exhausted. At that point there's nothing I enjoy more than a simple meal served in the family room, a fat copy of the *Chicago Tribune*, and a televised Chicago Bears football game. With my kids playing nearby and my wife curled up in an easy chair with a good book, the scene is complete. I usually drift off to sleep during the fourth quarter, and wake up just in time to have a light snack before "60 Minutes" comes on. After that, I greet my weekly discipleship group. For the next two hours we study and memorize Scripture, share personal needs, and pray and laugh and cry together.

By the time I go to bed on Sunday night, I feel as though I've enjoyed a slice of heaven. My body, mind, and spirit are relaxed, and I look forward to the coming week.

Perhaps your idea of a "perfect" Sabbath Day differs radically from mine. Maybe you'd prefer to take a walk, ride a bike, play a game, go on a picnic, get together with friends, or any one of a thousand other things. But whatever we choose to do, isn't it great to know we have freedom in Christ?

God wants us to honor the Sabbath by refraining from work, focusing on worship, and engaging in activities that contribute to our physical, emotional, and spiritual renewal. Does that sound like a burdensome command to you?

God asks so little of us, and gives so much in return. Why not honor Him on the Sabbath? Why not adapt your lifestyle to His divinely ordained schedule? You have nothing to lose—and so much to gain!

Five
Fulfill the Cycle of Love

"Honor your father and your mother, that your days may be prolonged in the land which the Lord your God gives you" (Exodus 20:12).

Entering into a proper relationship with God through Jesus Christ should be our highest priority. Why? Because that relationship affects every other aspect of our lives—both in our day-to-day earthly existence, and in the afterlife. A relationship with God is more important than status, wealth, beauty, brains, power, or any other temporal possession we might desire. All those things will fade—they'll rust, rot, and depreciate. But our relationship with God will endure forever.

As we have seen, this special relationship is the subject of the first four commandments. They teach us how to relate properly to God by giving Him first place in our lives, worshiping Him in spirit and in truth, reverencing His name, and honoring Him on the Sabbath. Only after thoroughly discussing our relationship with Himself does God move on to the fifth commandment, which addresses our relationships with others. He knows we must be at peace with Him and under the influence of His Spirit before we can hope to relate to others satisfactorily.

Occasionally, non-Christians come to me for counseling because they want to "get their act together" and work on family relationships. They're frustrated because their attempts to be more loving to family members usually end in failure. They can't forgive past wrongs. They can't overlook irritating habits. They can't love someone who seems "unlovable." They don't seem to have it in them. They just can't do it on their own.

I tell such people the same thing I tell myself every day of my life: "Of course you can't do it on your own! You need a love that's not your own—and a patient, forgiving spirit that's not your own. You need a change of heart."

Not long ago a friend of mine had to fire one of his key employees. "Five years ago, before I became a Christian, this would have been easy," he said. "I would have sent the guy a pink slip and said, 'Sorry, you weren't doing the job.' Short, simple, and to the point. This time, however, I agonized over the situation. As soon as I realized this man couldn't handle his responsibilities, I started praying about it. I even tried to alter his job description. But it just didn't work. I knew he had to go. So I flew to the city where his office was located and talked with him personally. I gave him my reasons and promised to help him find another position.

"It was easy to fire people when I didn't care about them. But now that I know the Lord, people and relationships are very important to me. I don't want to use or hurt people, or take their needs lightly. I want to love and encourage them."

That's exactly how every true believer should feel. As we grow in our relationship with God, we should experience a revolutionary change in our attitudes toward people. People should become more important to us. We should become more sensitive to their needs, desires, and hurts.

First Things First

God begins His discussion of human relationships by looking at the most basic social unit, the family. As always, He displays His divine wisdom by giving us a challenge that cuts to the core of our being. What relationships challenge us more than those we maintain over the course of an entire lifetime? And what relationship has more potential for both love and hate—and joy and sorrow—than the parent-child relationship?

Most experts agree that the family is the birthplace of self-esteem. In the family, children learn their value as human beings. They experiment with their interests, their abilities, and their intellects. They learn to relate to others. And they have the opportunity to see themselves through other people's eyes. As they do these things they develop a view of themselves—either negative or positive—based on their treatment within the family setting. Have they been accepted, encouraged, and praised? Or have they been ignored, belittled, and criticized? Their self-esteem probably will reflect the answers to those questions.

A properly functioning family also is the birthplace of respect for authority. Children learn in the family that certain lines must be drawn, certain expectations must be met, and certain people must be respected and obeyed. How a child learns about authority in the home will determine how he relates to teachers, coaches, employers, government officials, and ultimately, to God.

Finally, the home is the birthplace of values. By the time a child is a teenager he knows what's most important to his parents. He knows whether it's success in the marketplace, or pleasure, or money—or if it's relationships and obedience to Jesus Christ. And more likely than not, that teenager will carry those same values into his own adult life.

Obviously, some very important eggs are placed in the family basket. That's why God says so much about the family in Scripture. Many passages in the Psalms, Proverbs, and Epistles admonish parents to create a positive, godly family environment. Other passages, including the fifth commandment, turn the tables and admonish children to do *their* part in supporting a godly family structure. While parents have a responsibility to be loving, giving, conscientious authority figures, children have a duty to honor their parents in a God-glorifying way.

I suspect that God gave the fifth commandment because He knew how easy it would be for us to develop a disrespectful attitude toward our parents. As children, we're basically selfish; we want everything to go *our* way. As teenagers, we think our parents are hopelessly ignorant and "behind the times." As young adults, we become consumed with the responsibilities of work and marriage. And, as middle-aged adults, we view the needs of our aged parents as wearisome burdens that infringe on our hard-earned freedom.

This commandment tells us, however, that if we want to have a "right" relationship with God, we have to have a "right" relationship with our parents. We need to honor them the way God tells us to, whether we're younger children still living in our parents' home, or older children living on our own. But where do we begin?

In the Family Home

Children still living with their parents should begin with an attitude of cooperation toward their mother and father. Younger family members reading this book are probably grimacing already. But this matter of cooperation is not just my personal opinion. In Ephesians, Paul tells children to "obey your parents in the Lord, for this is right" (6:1). Godly obedience is not merely outward acquiescence accompanied by a grudging spirit. When God tells us to obey, He expects us to do it with a spirit of graciousness and cooperation.

Imagine a mother, father, and child taking a Sunday afternoon drive through the country. Five-year-old Johnny is standing in the seat between Mom and Dad, and they're all enjoying the fall scenery. As they approach a small town, Dad tells Johnny to sit down and put his seat belt on.

"No way, Dad," Johnny responds with unexpected defiance.

"Maybe you didn't understand me, Son," says Dad. "We're coming into heavy traffic and I want you to put your seat belt on."

Again Johnny refuses. "I don't want to, Dad. And I'm not gonna do it."

At this point Mom comes to the rescue and grabs Johnny's little earlobe. As she starts lowering him, she says, "Basically, what your dad means, Johnny, is that you either sit down and buckle up, or you're in big trouble!"

Wisely, Johnny sits down and buckles his seat belt. As he does so, however, he glares at his dad and mumbles, "I might be sitting down on the outside, but I'm standing up on the inside!"

Johnny gave mechanical compliance to his parents' order, but he did so in a state of inner rebellion. That's not what honoring our father and mother is all about.

When I come home from work and find the family room looking like a disaster area, with toys strewn from one end to the other, I have an impromtu business meeting with my kids. "Todd, Shauna," I say, "I think we have a little problem here. There's no excuse for a mess like this. I want you to pick up all the toys in this room and put them in the closet — *neatly*."

At that point, I'm not worried about whether the kids will pick up the toys. I know they will. I am concerned, however, about the attitude with which they'll perform this task. Sometimes Todd will pick up a little metal truck, take it over to the closet, and throw it into the box. Crash! Bang! Boom! In the process, he'll break two or three little plastic toys — and make it clear that it's time for us to have another little talk.

"Look, Buddy, it's not unfair for a father to ask his son to pick up his toys. I have to clean up my office after I do my work. Mom has to clean up the kitchen after she cooks dinner. And kids should pick up their toys after they play with them. In a family, everyone has to do his or her part. So don't get crabby when I ask you to do your share. Do it with a smile and a good attitude."

The Epistle to the Philippians tells us to "do all things without grumbling or disputing" (2:14). If you are still living with your parents, please take that verse to heart. Obey God and the fifth commandment by cooperating joyfully with your parents' requests. A grumbling spirit casts a dark shadow over the atmosphere of a home, whereas good-natured obedience is the surest way to ease tension and promote harmony.

The next time your parents ask you to help them with something — such as taking out the garbage, washing dishes, cleaning your room, or mowing the lawn — why not say, "Sure, I'd be glad to." That simple response probably will make your parents' day. And it will undoubtedly please the Lord.

Another way to honor one's parents is to show them respect. We honor God by addressing Him respectfully and using His name carefully. We should behave the same way toward our parents.

Many of the "macho" guys I hung around with in grade school called their parents "old man" and "old lady." As much as I wanted to please my peers, I never could bring myself to refer to my parents that way. I clearly remember being in the boys' lavatory one afternoon, when a guy several years older than myself came in. He spoke about his parents in a derogatory way, then said to me, "Hey, Hybels, what do you think of your old man and your old lady?"

I knew this guy was big enough to clean my clock, so I didn't try to interfere with his freedom of speech. In fact, as I remember, I gave him full permission to call my parents anything he wanted to. I did make it clear, however, that *I* had no intention of talking about my parents that way. They didn't deserve it, and I wasn't about to do it.

I challenge you to display an attitude of respect for your parents. Be careful how you talk to others about them. Address them respectfully. Listen courteously to their advice and opinions; they may have a wealth of insight and wisdom you've not yet acquired. And remember, parents are people with feelings — just like you. Don't abuse those feelings by displaying a disrespectful attitude.

Finally, we can honor our parents by being appreciative of what they've done for us. Most of us can honestly say that our parents have made a larger investment in our lives than anyone else. I didn't realize that ten years ago. But the experience of being a parent myself has taught me some valuable lessons.

When my wife became pregnant with our first child, she had no idea what was in store for her. She didn't know she would spend the next nine months fighting desperately to "keep her lunch down." She didn't know that the miraculous, yet traumatic, experience of childbirth would arouse such fears in her. She didn't know that nighttime feedings, dirty diapers, and interrupted plans would be so over-whelming.

Nor did I know how drastically children would alter our life-style. Or how hard it would be to coordinate family needs and ministry needs. Or how challenging the role of being a father would be.

It has been estimated that it will cost the average parents as much as $250,000 to raise one child from infancy to eighteen years of age. But that monetary investment is nothing compared to the investment of time, concern, prayer, and planning that most parents put into their child-rearing practices. My wife and I discuss our children more frequently than any other subject. How can we best meet their needs? How can we stimulate their minds? How can we build their self-esteem? How can we help them uncover their strengths and abilities?

Parents have to grapple with these and many other issues. Because we're imperfect, we make mistakes and have regrets. But the fact remains that we make a tremendous investment in the lives of our children. Our love for them demands it.

What's the best way to crush your parents' spirit? Just neglect to show appreciation for what they do. Keep on taking, taking, taking, without ever saying "thank you" — without ever showing gratitude.

On the other hand, what's the best way to lift your parents' spirits? Show a little appreciation. You don't have to get fancy. Just say, "Thanks for preparing that meal. It was great." Or, "I really appreciate the way you do my laundry." Or, "It's nice of you to pick me up from school."

When my kids thank me for simple things, it makes a tremendous difference in my attitude toward parenting. It motivates me to make even greater investments in their lives. The same thing happens when they obey me without an argument or display an attitude of respect. When they honor me, they encourage me to be the best parent I can be.

Every day, you have hundreds of opportunities to show your parents obedience, respect, and appreciation. Why not take advantage of them? Your parents will benefit by it—and so will you!

Outside the Parental Home

Some people think the fifth commandment applies only to children living in their parents' home. But I believe it applies across the board. Even if we live outside our parental home and support ourselves—and even if we have new families of our own—we are still commanded to honor our parents.

A marvelous cycle is evident in the ongoing life of a family. When a baby is born into a family, he is totally dependent on his parents. As he grows, he becomes increasingly independent, until one day he is ready to leave the home of his youth and establish one of his own. He has followed the God-ordained path to maturity.

His parents, meanwhile, have followed another path designed by God—a path that has taken them from the vitality of youth and the security of middle age to the vulnerability of the aged. In that final state of vulnerability, they become dependent on the children they have raised, and the cycle is complete.

I've personally seen this cycle illustrated at its best in my wife's family. For years, Lynne's mother has provided at-home care for her own invalid mother. Lynne and I often have made special plans with Lynne's parents, only to have them interrupted by Grandma's needs. And repeatedly over the years, Lynne's father has had to alter his lifestyle to make room for his aged mother-in-law.

Compared to the treatment most elderly parents receive in this society, Lynne's grandmother has been treated wonderfully. But it's even more amazing when you realize that her family has helped her without the slightest hint of complaint or resentment. While Lynne and her brother were growing up, they considered it a privilege to have Grandma with them all the time. They thought they were the luckiest kids in the neighborhood. They cherished the special relationship they enjoyed with her. Lynne's mother thought it was only natural to provide a warm and loving home for the woman who had done the same for her many years earlier. She was grateful for the opportunity to show her appreciation and preserve her mother's dignity in her old age. Likewise, Lynne's dad believed that God had called him to support his wife in this endeavor, and he did so graciously.

What a testimony of love this has been to me. Each time we visit Lynne's parents' home in Michigan, we see that love enacted again. At ninety-two, Grandma is still a major focus of concern.

One of the elders in our church provided another vivid illustration of obedience to the fifth commandment. Every morning at 6:00 he went to the nursing home where his mother lived. There he bathed her, prayed with her, and joined her in singing the old hymns of faith she loved. He could have waited for the nurses to bathe her at 11:00, as was required on their work order. And he could have relied on the weekly church services to meet his mother's spiritual needs. But he thought she deserved more than that; so he took it on himself to provide it. When she died, he knew he had done all he could to add joy to her life.

We also see this loving concern illustrated in the life of Jesus. Even during His time of greatest need, our Lord turned His attention toward His mother. Imagine Him on the cross, hanging naked between heaven and earth with the weight of our sin on His shoulders. For an instant, Jesus opens His eyes and sees His mother. He knows how much she'll miss the support of her eldest son; so He asks John to care for her—as a mother. John obviously knew what his master meant, for Scripture tells us that "from that hour the disciple took her into his own household" (John 19:27).

Often, our excuse for not caring for our parents is that we don't have time. But even Jesus took time to make sure His mother was properly cared for, and we should do no less.

Some of us will have the opportunity and the wherewithal to have our aged parents live in our homes once they get to the point of dependence. Others of us will never be called on to do that, will not have the resources to do it, or will have a more satisfactory option available. But whatever the situation, we should follow some practical suggestions in caring for our aged parents.

First, we must make sure their basic needs are met. Jesus viciously attacked the Pharisees because they taught people to give money to the temple that should have been used to support their parents (Matt. 15:4-6). How could the Pharisees demand money for God's work—and undoubtedly for their own pockets—at the expense of needy elderly parents? To Jesus, this was unthinkable.

We must make sure our parents have food, housing, clothes, medical care, and every other basic necessity of life. If those needs have been met, we can further support our parents by helping with mundane—but often overwhelming—household responsibilities. We can put up storm windows, fix a fence, mow the lawn, repair their car, handle legal responsibilities, etc. A small commitment of our time and energy can greatly reduce the stress and frustration of aging.

Another practical suggestion is to include older parents in a wide variety of family activities. We often have postponed birthday parties for days—even weeks—in order to coordinate celebrations with both sets of out-of-state grandparents. We may give the children a "token" present on their birthday, but they know the real celebration will happen when Grandma and Grandpa arrive. Easter, Thanksgiving, and Christmas also are special extended family times for us. Occasionally, extenuating circumstances keep us from following this prescribed pattern, but those times definitely are the exception rather than the rule.

Several months after my father died, I was asked to teach for a week at a school in the Dominican Republic. As an honorarium, the school offered to send Lynne, the kids, and me to the island of St. Croix for a week-long vacation. Because my mother was still grieving and was experiencing the unfamiliar loneliness of widowhood, Lynne and I invited her to make the trip with us. Not only did we benefit from the added bonus of having a built-in baby-sitter along on the trip, but my mother and I enjoyed a level of friendship we had not previously experienced. It was a memorable vacation for all of us.

Many gracious people in our church have offered to let us use their vacation homes in exotic locations during my summer study break. As tempting as these opportunities are, we're repeatedly drawn back to a tiny, one-bedroom cottage on the eastern shore of Lake Michigan. Why? Because it's about two blocks from my mother's summer home and two miles from the marina where my father-in-law moors his sailboat. We thoroughly enjoy traveling and seeing the world, but when it comes to an extended vacation, we'd rather be with family. Our kids benefit immeasurably from the time they spend with their grandparents, and the grandparents view it as the highlight of their year.

Make it a point to include aged parents in special family times. It tells them they're important. It seals their place in the family structure. And it sets the stage for a healthy mix of ages that enriches all our lives.

A third suggestion is to communicate and affirm our love for our parents on a regular basis. Someday you're going to get a phone call similar to the one I received five years ago. When I answered the phone I heard nothing but silence for a few seconds, then my brother said, "Billy, I'm sorry to have to tell you this—but Dad died this morning."

The first thing that went through my mind when I heard those words was, "Oh, I'm so glad he knew I loved him." I thought about his recent visit when we stood in my garage and talked about things that were important to us. I thought about the trips we had taken together over the years. I thought about the phone calls halfway across the world.

The day after my dad passed away, my brother and I began cleaning out the desk in his office. Note pads, files, and stacks of legal documents attested to the scope of his business responsibilities. But in the top drawer on the right- hand side, I found a collection of letters that seemed to occupy a position of honor. There, neatly grouped in rubber bands, were all the letters my brother and sisters and I had ever written to my dad.

I flipped through the stack and found the scribbled notes I had sent him from college. One said nothing but "Thanks for the rich heritage you have given me." Another confessed, "If I can be half the father to my kids that you have been to me, my life will be a smashing success." Another simply remarked, "Thanks for taking the time to visit me last weekend. I had a great time."

I realized then how important it is for children to communicate their love and appreciation to their parents. My dad's business files were carelessly scattered from one end of his office to the other. But the written affirmations of his children's love were cherished, protected, and kept close at hand.

When was the last time you told your parents you love them? When was the last time you sent a note? I'm sure it's not too soon to do it again.

Children living in the parental home should honor their parents by cooperating with them joyfully, respecting them, and expressing appreciation. Children living outside the family home should make sure their parents' basic needs are met, ought to include them in family activities, and should communicate their love to them over and over again.

Our reward for obeying the fifth commandment will be the blessing of a warm and harmonious family life—and that is a rich blessing indeed. When we're enjoying a right relationship with God and a right relationship with our parents, we have the most important relationships in life in order—and the freedom to establish a right relationship with the world.

Destroy the Killer in You

"You shall not murder" (Exodus 20:13).

Tourists who visit Chicago today can travel down Lake Shore Drive and pass beaches and sparkling harbors dotted with bright sails. Others can enjoy nature's bounteous displays at the Chicago Botanic Gardens or the Brookfield Zoo. Still others can view man's achievements at the Art Institute and the Museum of Science and Industry. From the spectacular Lake Michigan skyline to Buckingham Fountain to the famed Gold Coast, there is beauty for the seeking.

Unfortunately, however, other aspects of Chicago's reputation are not as proudly hailed. The city renowned for its beauty also is infamous for its crooked politics, its shady union bosses, and its busy hit men.

Murder, Chicago-style

I remember the first time I heard the term, "Chicago-style murder." While reading an East Coast newspaper, I came across headlines announcing a gruesome gangland slaying. A subtitle called the murder a "Chicago-style hit."

The beautiful city on the lake first earned this aspect of its reputation during the Al Capone era of the 20s and 30s. But a wide variety of underground figures have conscientiously perpetuated it. Chicago is still one of the "contract capitals" of the world, and its citizens continue to make national headlines by inflicting multiple gunshot wounds on one another, hiding dead bodies in car trunks, and using "cement slippers" to assure former friends a place at the bottom of the Chicago River.

But we all know that it's not fair to pick solely on Chicago. Chicago-style murders are nothing new, and they're certainly not confined to the Windy City. Throughout history, men and women have been wielding rocks, knives, axes, swords, and spears against their neighbors. Whether they've been motivated by anger, hatred, greed, fear, or jealousy, the outcome often has been the same—murder.

The first biblically recorded homicide is described in Genesis 4. In a fit of jealousy and anger, Adam's firstborn son, Cain, slew his brother Abel. Imagine the horror of the scene. No living being had ever witnessed the awful spectacle of human death. Yet there before Adam and Eve lay the cold, lifeless body of their son—flesh of their flesh and bone of their bone.

Imagine the questions that raced through their minds. *Cain, how could you? How dare you? What right did you have to decide that Abel should die? You're not God!*

Such questions reveal the heinous nature of murder. God creates and sustains man, and He alone has the right to number his days. When humans pirate God's prerogative to control life and death, they commit an unspeakable offense before God, the victim, and society. The sixth commandment says no one but God has the right to determine when a person should die.

Surely, this law also applies to suicide and abortion, as well as to willful acts of violence that stop short of death. At this point in history child abuse has become a national nightmare, and battered wives keep hot lines busy and shelters full. Statistics tell us that unprecedented numbers of Americans live in private torture chambers, where violence is passed from one generation to the next. Can we doubt the need for a prohibition against violence?

Even professional athletes often use unnecessary violence. It's pretty hard to justify the fighter who turns his opponent's face into a bloody mask, and then says jubilantly, "I just wanted to pound his head in!" But we don't even let it bother us. Similarly, we leave hockey games disappointed if we don't see a brawl, and we closely watch the late night news to see recaps of the day's sporting violence.

After the news, we let the late night movie chill us with true-to-life horror stories. And we corporately pour billions of dollars into a film industry that turns violence into entertainment.

All the while, God points to the sixth commandment and says, "Don't you understand? I have a better plan. I don't want men to sleep with pistols under their pillows. I don't want women to carry mace in their purses. I don't want every door in every house to be triple-locked. My people shouldn't have to live that way. So don't kill each other. Don't abuse one another. And don't condone violence. Please, please, please—obey the sixth commandment!"

More Than One Way to Murder a Man

At first glance, the sixth commandment appears to be the easiest of the ten to obey. Most of us have never killed anyone and certainly don't intend to. So why waste time addressing this issue? Why not move on to commandment number seven?

Well, before we decide we're free to bypass this commandment, perhaps we should hear what Jesus had to say about it:

> You have heard that the ancients were told, "You shall not commit murder" and "Whoever commits murder shall be liable to the court." But I say to you that every one who is angry with his brother shall be guilty before the court; and whoever shall say to his brother, "Raca," shall be guilty before the supreme court; and whoever

shall say, "You fool," shall be guilty enough to go into the hell of fire (Matt. 5:21-22).

In simple terms, Jesus was telling us there's more than one way to murder a man. And I think He'd say the same thing today. He'd tell those of us who live in nice neighborhoods, who work for nice companies, and who attend nice churches, that there are murderers in our midst. Oh, they may not be Chicago-style murderers; but they are killers, nonetheless.

Suburban-style Murders

Most people who read this book are far too civilized and controlled to participate in Chicago-style slayings. Sophisticated suburbanites that we are, we use our guns for show or target practice. We use our knives to cut our gourmet quiche. The only slippers we're familiar with are the ones we step into en route to our easy chairs.

Oh yes, we're a far different breed from the Chicago-style killers. But I wouldn't be surprised if we're exactly the kind of people Jesus spoke to in Matthew (5:21-22). We wouldn't think of lifting a gun or a knife against another person, but we destroy them just the same. We harbor unresolved anger that displays itself in a hateful attitude toward others. Or, like Jesus' contemporaries, we question other men's worth by calling them *raca* — good for nothing. And what does Jesus say about people who do these things? That they are worthy of hell — just like murderers.

In this passage, Jesus reveals the striking similarity between physical and verbal violence. There is little difference between a dripping knife and juicy gossip, between racing bullets and an abusive tongue. Why? Because they all flow from the same source — a hateful heart. And they all kill. When Chicago-style murderers kill, they usurp God's right to number a man's days. When suburban-style murderers kill, they usurp God's right to measure a man's worth.

Man, created in God's image, is the crown of all Creation. He is God's masterpiece, His most priceless possession. As such, he has great value—not, of course, because he deserves it—but because God chooses to value him. That is an indisputable and blessed biblical truth. God deems man valuable, precious, worthy.

Who are we, then, to decide that some men are not worthy, or precious, or valuable? Who are we to decide that they can be called a loser, or fool, or nigger, or spick, or chink? What right do we have to crush their spirits by insulting them, humiliating them, or discriminating against them? We have *no* right to do those things—absolutely none!

Before I started working on this chapter, I assumed that I'd be able to stand guiltless before the sixth commandment. I now realize that all too often I've adopted the role of the suburban-style murderer. With careless insensitivity, and sometimes even malice, I've ripped people to shreds with my words. And I stand before God guilty, desperately needing His forgiveness.

Do you too need to confess the sin of murder? If we're serious about honoring God, we must be serious about dealing with the sixth commandment. James tells us that with the same tongue we "bless our Lord and Father; and with it we curse men, who have been made in the likeness of God; from the same mouth come both blessing and cursing. My brethren, *these things ought not to be this way*" (3:9; emphasis mine). We can't use our mouths to worship God one minute, and then use them to abuse men the next.

Perhaps we need to look back in history to a bloodstained cross. Perhaps we need to look again at a dying Savior who had every right to curse us for violating His Father's holiness with our sin. Yes, He had the right to do that. But what did He do instead? He looked at us through the eyes of unfathomable love, took our sins on Himself, and freed us from the doom of eternal death.

Jesus wasn't forced to do that. He *chose* to do it because He loved us. And now He wants to pour that same love into our hearts so we can show it to others. King David earnestly begged

God to create in him a clean heart and to renew his spirit (Ps. 51:10). We have to do that as well. We need to ask God to replace the hatred in our hearts with love, the arrogance with humility, the bitterness with tolerance, and the malice with understanding. We need a nonviolent heart so we can speak nonviolent words.

O Father, forgive us for being suburban-style killers. Purify us so we can obey Your command.

Religious-style Murderers

Chicago-style killers are a brash bunch. Their crimes are gruesome, easy to detect, and deadly. Suburban-style killers are more subtle, and their crimes less visible; but their attacks are just as direct — and just as deadly. There's a third type of killer, however, whose methods differ drastically from the others'. These killers commit no murderous acts, and use neither their hands nor their tongues. They kill simply by neglect and apathy. They kill by withholding that which sustains life — love and attention.

Of course, these people would never call themselves killers. But that's exactly what they are — pious, self-righteous, religious-style killers. And Jesus condemned them to the fate all unrepentant murderers deserve. Why? The reason is found in Christ's own words:

> I was hungry, and you gave Me nothing to eat; I was thirsty, and you gave Me nothing to drink; I was a stranger, and you did not invite Me in; naked, and you did not clothe Me; sick, and in prison, and you did not visit Me (Matt. 25:42-43).

"I know you didn't plunge a sword into My side, as a Chicago-style killer would have done," Jesus is saying. "And I know you didn't make fun of Me, as a suburban-style killer would have. But you gave Me no food when I was hungry. You gave

Me no coat when I was cold. So I died. There was no sword, no slander—but no help, either. And now My blood is on your hands."

Our church periodically sponsors food drives. On a given Sunday morning, church members bring in bags of groceries which are used to stock the shelves of our church-operated Food Pantry. The Pantry then distributes the food to needy families in our church and community. Another portion of the food is distributed to disadvantaged families in the inner city. We also do the same thing with used clothing.

Most people in our church wholeheartedly support these programs. In fact, they look forward to expanding this particular ministry. But I know that each time I announce a food or clothing drive, a few individuals think, *Oh boy, here we go again—another handout request. Why do they keep begging me for help? I work hard. I pay my bills. I take care of my family. Let those other people do the same. They're not my responsibility.*

If you find yourself echoing those words, maybe you need to take another look at a dying Savior. Maybe you need a new heart. I'm well acquainted with man's natural tendency to isolate himself in his own little world and ignore the needy. How easy it is for me to say, "Hey, I've got my loving wife, my precious kids, my Malibu station wagon, and my cozy home in the suburbs. This is my world. If people outside it are hungry and naked and dying . . . well, I hope somebody takes care of them."

I recognize those thoughts. And I know they grieve the heart of God. Over and over again I've had to confess the hardness of my heart and admit that I'm a pious killer. No swords. No slander. But no help.

The Apostle John says, "But whoever has the world's goods, and beholds his brother in need and closes his heart against him, how does the love of God abide in him?" (1 John 3:17) Something is dreadfully wrong with a believer who has an apathetic heart. When we withhold our help from those who desperately need it—whether that help takes a spiritual, emotional, or physical form—we belie the sickness of our own hearts.

As I said earlier, when I started working on this chapter, I thought this commandment was going to be a breeze. As it turned out, this has been the most personally challenging section for me so far. I've been forced to admit that far too often I slip into the role of a killer. How I pray that God will transform me daily, and change the hatred in my heart to love, the violence to tenderness, the slander to encouragement, the apathy to a God-inspired activism.

Are you willing to let God destroy the killer in you? Do you dare yield your heart to His transforming power? Will you commit yourself to using your hands for tenderness, your words for encouragement, and your resources for the good of the needy? Will you?

Seven
Keep Pleasure Undefiled

"You shall not commit adultery" (Exodus 20:14).

"Hi, Madam. I'm Adam."

No, no, no. He wouldn't have said anything that corny.

"Howdy, Ma'am. Pleased to meet ya."

Oh, come on. He wasn't filming a western movie.

Well, maybe he just gave her a mischievous little smile. Or perhaps he just whistled at her. Who knows? What would *you* have done if you were Adam meeting Eve for the first time?

Picture the scene. Adam's wandering around in a gigantic garden, picking berries and talking to animals. It's a lovely day, and he's enjoying the scenery; but he *is* starting to feel a bit lonely. His loneliness, however, hasn't escaped the notice of the all-knowing God.

"Hey, Adam," God says, "I have a little surprise for you. I've been waiting for just the right time, and I think this is it. You take a little nap, and when you wake up, you're going to have a real treat waiting for you!"

While Adam sleeps, God takes one of his ribs and fashions it into a woman; He then breathes into her nostrils the breath of life. When Adam awakes, she's waiting for him—living, breathing, shapely, long-haired Eve.

What do you think Adam did at that point? The Bible only tells us that he called her "bone of my bone, and flesh of my flesh" (Gen. 2:23), but I think that simple statement reveals the depth of his identification with her. Here at last was one who was like him, someone with whom he could share all things, with whom he could commune at the deepest level.

God revealed His view of Adam and Eve's special companionship when He said, "For this cause a man shall leave his father and mother, and shall cleave to his wife; and they shall become one flesh" (Gen. 2:24). This man and woman were to have a unique relationship, a relationship in which they would be joined together in the flesh, beautifully and intimately, in a way ordained by God.

You've Got to Be Kidding!

Some people are shocked to learn that God is "pro-sex." Having heard so many erroneous analyses of God's view of sex, they find it hard to accept the truth—that the Holy God of Israel, the author of the Ten Commandments, is the foremost proponent of healthy sex.

Yet Scripture clearly reveals this fact. We learn from the Creation account that the sexual dimension of our personality is woven into the very fabric of who we are as human beings. Physiologically and psychologically, we are created to be sexual beings. The physical attraction between male and female was no accident, and it certainly was not the result of evil. It was a beautiful and important part of God's wise design.

Furthermore, Scripture seems to indicate that God created human sexuality primarily for pleasure. Procreation appears to be a secondary purpose. God first spoke of man and woman "becoming one flesh" within the context of ending Adam's isolation and loneliness (Gen. 2:18-25); the role of procreation is not mentioned until later.

We see a "pro-sex" attitude not only in Genesis, but in the

rest of the Bible as well. The Song of Solomon is a poetic description of the romantic and erotic attraction between two lovers. Many commentators view it as a reflection of what Adam may have felt when God provided Eve as his wife. The *Open Bible*, for example, says in its introduction to the Song of Solomon:

> In frank but pure language the book praises the mutual love between husband and wife, and thereby teaches us not to despise physical beauty and married love as being of a low order. Since these are gifts from the Creator to His creatures (cf. James 1:17), they are good and perfect in their place and for their purpose (p. 619).

The Apostle Paul also tells married couples not to deprive one another of sex, but to engage in it regularly. This rule, he says, has only one exception: By *mutual agreement*, a couple may abstain from sex for a brief period of time while they devote themselves more fully to prayer (1 Cor. 7:5).

We know that God is "pro-sex." We know that Scripture is "pro-sex." Now, doesn't it follow that Christians should be "pro-sex"? Why should we deny a God-designed dimension of our human makeup?

Several years ago I counseled a couple whose marriage was headed for disaster. Their major problem was that both husband and wife had grown up under a pastor who believed that sex was inherently evil. His viewpoint so distorted their perception of sex, that they didn't even engage in it until several months after their wedding. And when they did, the experience was surrounded by guilt and shame. This problem continued to plague them through their fifteen-year marriage.

How tragic that such a dark shadow can be cast over a dimension of life that God designed to be beautiful. But, while tragic, it really should come as no surprise; we seem to be masters at shading and distorting the beautiful things God has created. In fact, it appears that anything God can create, man can pervert.

God created a world filled with beauty for man to enjoy and resources for him to use. But what has man done? He's gotten greedy and careless; in the name of progress, he's blighted nature's beauty and stripped her resources.

God created within man an appetite for food and drink. He wanted man to sustain himself nutritionally, and to enjoy the vast array of delicious foods that He provided. But what has man done? All too often, he has abused this natural desire for food and drink, and paid for his abuse through obesity or drunkenness.

The same often is true with sex. God designed the sexual relationship to bind two people together as one flesh; but men and women have perverted it. They have used this most intimate human experience to shatter personalities and destroy families. Some people have done this by calling sex evil, and denying men and women the joy God intended them to share. Others have done it by going to the opposite extreme, and ignoring the parameters that God has placed around the sexual experience. They have removed sex from its sacred bounds and opened a Pandora's box of devastating consequences.

That is precisely why God gave us the seventh commandment. He wanted to make sure sex always would be a tool for unity, not for division. He wanted to keep it beautiful by keeping it pure and undefiled. The seventh commandment is not my law, nor is it merely a human opinion sanctioned by church tradition. It is God's direct provision for protecting His creation. By logical extension, it covers the three most common forms of sexual perversion—adultery, fornication, and lust.

The Marriage Bed Defiled

God created a full spectrum of sexual pleasures for us to enjoy, but they are to be enjoyed only within the context of marriage. That is the basic message of the seventh commandment.

God knows that sex is a risky business. He knows that men and women are never more vulnerable than when they lay naked in bed with one another. On the one hand, in such situations, they long to take off their masks and disclose themselves fully—their feelings, their thoughts, their physical drives. On the other hand, they fear that total exposure will destroy their fragile world of love; they might be rejected, scorned, or misunderstood.

Yes, sex is a risky business. That's why God confines it to marriage, where a covenant has been made, where a lifelong commitment has been promised. In that environment, trust and security can grow, and gradually fear, anxiety, and inhibition can subside. For sex to be all God intended it to be, it must occur in a marriage relationship based on solid communication patterns, mutual devotion, respect, confidentiality, and above all, absolute loyalty. Only in that kind of relational environment can we expect to have a truly satisfying sexual experience.

My wife and I have found that our level of sexual enjoyment always is proportionate to the *overall* quality of our marriage. Sex counselors too affirm that basic truth. The sexual dimension of marriage often can be viewed as a barometer of the level of tension or harmony that exists in other areas of the marriage. A poor physical relationship may indicate broken communication patterns or a lack of devotion, respect, and trust. A healthy physical relationship probably indicates open communication lines and a high degree of warmth, loyalty, and mutual support. Sex is so much more than just physical intercourse. It is a God-ordained means of communicating love, a mutually enjoyable means of sealing a commitment, and the ultimate expression of vulnerability and trust.

Against that backdrop, we can see why adultery is such a serious offense. A person who commits this sin is not just violating an oath. He is violating another person. It is not the adulterous sexual relationship, itself, that is so destructive; it is the accompanying deceit, dishonesty, and disloyalty that shatter marriages and threaten the self-esteem of the violated partner.

"How could you deceive me like this?" a husband or wife asks. "How could you lie and mock my trust?"

That's where the agony comes in. And it's an agony that's almost unbearable. I had been in the ministry for only two years when I had to sit down with a young father and help him tell his two little children that Mommy wasn't coming home anymore; she had moved away with another man. The pain of that experience burned its way into my mind so deeply that I hoped never to get involved in another situation like that again. But I *have* gotten involved. Why? Because over the years men and women have continued to violate their spouses. And violated, broken spouses have continued to knock on the door to my office.

Hollywood makes the free and easy lifestyle of adultery appear so glamorous. But it's a blatant lie. *Adultery causes pain*. Everybody loses. Everybody suffers. Everybody is scarred. If adultery leads to divorce, as it so often does, the pain can last a lifetime.

God wants to spare us this pain. He wants to protect us, our spouses, and our families. He wants our marriages to be pure and undefiled, havens of love, trust, warmth, and pleasure. He wants sex to be a tool for building unity into our marriages — not a weapon for destroying it.

Please don't toy with the seventh commandment. Take it seriously. Obey it. And carefully consider these six practical suggestions for protecting your marriage.

(1) If you're not already married, decide that you'll only marry another Christian. From cover to cover, the Bible warns of the dangers of believers marrying unbelievers (2 Cor. 6:14). As a pastor, I've seen many Christian young people ignore this warning — and suffer the consequences later. They thought everything would work out fine because "they really loved each other," their future spouse would "become a Christian soon," or they were "mature enough to handle it." But they were wrong and had to pay the price. Please don't do that.

(2) Center your life on Jesus Christ and devote yourself to His Word. Make spiritual growth a priority and give the Holy Spirit a chance to mold you into a godly man or woman, husband or wife.

(3) Carefully follow every biblical guideline for improving your marriage. Seek sound teaching from the Word of God. Read books and listen to tapes on marriage and family. Be willing to put time and energy into building your marriage.

(4) Make your spouse a priority. Be interested in his or her concerns. Develop intimacy outside the bedroom by communicating openly and frequently. Continue the process of "getting to know one another" that began in courtship. Set aside time for regularly scheduled "date nights." Lynne and I attribute much of the health of our marriage to our weekly night out.

(5) Meet your partner's sexual needs so completely that he or she will have no desire to look elsewhere. I cannot overstate the importance of this point. It is vital that we know what our spouses need from us sexually, and that we do our best to meet those needs. This requires sensitivity, communication, and a willingness to give of ourselves to our spouses.

(6) Avoid relationships that might tempt you to commit adultery. I must confess that some women attract me just a little bit more than they ought to. Because of that, I cautiously avoid certain types of contact with them. I don't meet with them in my office. I don't suggest that we have lunch together. I don't even talk with them alone in the church lobby. I want to keep a wall of protection around myself. Why? Because I love my wife and I want to honor my commitment to her. I don't want to hurt her. And I don't want to do anything to jeopardize the deep level of trust and security that has developed in our marriage over the past ten years. I would be a fool to do that!

Not the Unpardonable Sin

Some people undoubtedly suffered from sweaty palms and churning stomachs as they read this chapter. Why? Because in their minds they carry the unburied memory of their own adulterous sin. If that describes you, please read these next words carefully. *God's grace is bigger than your sin. Jesus' blood can cleanse you and He is willing to forgive you.*

There is no reason for you to carry a burden of guilt for adultery committed in the past. Right now you can confess your sin to God and claim His forgiveness. God always offers mercy to a repentant sinner. When Jesus met the woman caught in adultery, He didn't condemn her. He sensed her repentant spirit and said, "Go your way; from now on sin no more" (John 8:11).

That's the same thing He's saying to you. So confess your sin, ask God's forgiveness, and then commit yourself to faithfulness in your marriage.

I can't guarantee that your spouse will have the same forgiving spirit God has. I can say, however, that I've had the pleasure of seeing more than one violated partner forgive a repentant spouse. I have witnessed firsthand the complete rebuilding of a destroyed marriage, as both husband and wife committed themselves to restoring a foundation of trust and respect and loyalty. This didn't happen overnight. And it could never have occurred without the intervention of God's healing Spirit. But it did happen. And it can happen to other people who are willing to repent and forgive.

The Popular Sin

Some people assume that the only sexual prohibition in the Bible is the one against adultery. They believe unmarried people can legitimately engage in sexual activities as long as their partner also is not married. I hate to rain on their parade, but I have to tell them that they're categorically wrong. Obviously, they haven't worn out their Bibles looking for instruction on sexual relationships!

The biblical term for premarital sex—any sex engaged in by unmarried persons—is fornication, and Scripture explicitly prohibits it. Matthew lists fornication right after murder and adultery (15:19), and Ephesians tells us that sexual immorality shouldn't even be mentioned as an option among Christians (5:3). It should be the farthest thing from our minds. Sex belongs in marriage, and *only* in marriage.

Remember, God wants sexual activity to be enjoyed within the context of a secure, permanent relationship. Bed-hopping is a gross distortion of God's plan. It strips the sexual relationship of the one-to-one intimacy that makes it special and valuable. It separates sex from the loving commitment that gives it meaning.

But some people will say, "You don't understand. We're not bed-hopping. We're not running from partner to partner. We're not buying sex. We're in love and we plan to be married someday. Why shouldn't we enjoy sex now?"

Jesus said that if we love Him, we'll keep His commandments (John 14:15). To young people who use their mutual love to justify their mutual sin, I can only say this: Who do you love more? God or your partner? Are you willing to disavow your love for the Lord for the sake of your future spouse—or for the sake of your own pleasure?

Sex is not dirty, ugly, or evil. It's beautiful, pure, and holy— but only when it's enjoyed by people who love God and are willing to obey the guidelines He has established. I'm convinced this commandment is given for our own good. I believe God wants to protect single people from life-threatening diseases and unwanted pregnancies. And I believe He wants to protect them from the emotional pain that results when they naively place their fragile self-esteem in the hands of those who can't be trusted.

If you're involved in a relationship tainted by sexual sin, God would implore you to repent immediately and commit yourself to sexual purity. Again, fornication is not the unpardonable sin. God will forgive you, cleanse you, and free you from the burden of guilt. He'll also give you the strength to abstain from sexual activities until you're married.

After you commit yourself to purity before God, announce that decision to your partner. Don't discuss it. Don't solicit his or her opinion on the matter. You'll never go through with it if you ask for a vote. Just announce your decision and your reason—obedience to God.

Several years ago, a couple with no previous church background visited our worship service. My message that day was a simple explanation of the Gospel, and apparently, its basic truths made sense to this couple. Within weeks, both had accepted Christ as their Savior. They then came to my office to ask a few questions and to get some reading material. During the course of our conversation I learned that they had been living together for seven years, unmarried, in a home they had purchased jointly.

Their hearts sank when I told them their living arrangement was not pleasing to God. If they really meant business with God, they would have to make a change.

The woman acknowledged that the Lord meant more to her than her living arrangements, and decided to move out. Her boyfriend agreed with her decision and made arrangements for her to move in with his parents. They then established a pattern of sexual purity which they maintained until their marriage almost a year later.

They've been married two years now, and it's obvious God's hand is on them. They readily admit that the turning point in their relationship and in their spiritual lives was the day they decided to become sexually pure. I challenge those of you who are living in sexual sin to follow their example.

It Starts in the Heart

Jesus said, "You have heard that it was said, 'You shall not commit adultery'; but I say to you, that everyone who looks on a woman to lust for her has committed adultery with her already in his heart" (Matt. 5:27-28).

In this message to the multitude, Jesus did what He had done so many times before. He looked behind an outward expression of sin and saw its inner manifestation. While the outward expression of sexual impurity is adultery or fornication, the inner manifestation is lust. To many people lust seems innocent — or if not quite innocent, at least not worth mentioning. After all, they say, its only playground is the mind. But what happens in the mind *is important* — very important — for it is in the mind that the battle for sexual purity must be fought.

All of us notice attractive members of the opposite sex now and then. Attraction and stimulation are normal reactions for sexual beings, such as we are. Obviously, that normal reaction does not constitute the lust to which Jesus referred in Matthew 5.

No, it's not the first, casual look that constitutes lust. Nor is it the innocent appreciation of a muscular physique, a shapely body, or a pretty face. It's the second, third, or fourth look — the look that's accompanied by an imagined seduction, a mental undressing, and a conscious fantasy of having a sexual relationship with that person — that defines lust. That is what Jesus forbade.

A mind that persistently dreams and schemes and seduces is a mind that needs cleansing. Jesus calls lust "adultery in the heart," and like any other sexual sin, it must be confessed and abandoned. If we don't confess and turn away from it, it eventually will consume our thoughts. And if we encourage it with sexually stimulating films, books, magazines, or social settings, we'll probably yield to the temptation — and turn the fantasy into reality.

Please don't do that. Don't fill your mind with garbage. When we flirt with sin, we eventually fall prey to it — and then we have to pay the price of disobedience.

As I've indicated repeatedly throughout this book, God loves us and wants to liberate us. That's why He gave us the seventh commandment. He wants to free our minds from the shadow of sin so that we can think constructively, worship joyfully, and relate to other people in pure and healthy ways. He doesn't want to deny us the pleasures of life. He simply wants to keep our pleasures undefiled.

Eight
Acquire by the Rules

"You shall not steal" (Exodus 20:15).

It was Christmas Eve. My sister, Ginny, was driving home from a late night service at her church. The trees lining the country road glistened momentarily as they caught the beam of her headlights. The wet snowflakes gathered in icy mounds on her windshield wipers and left a thin layer of slippery moisture on the narrow road. As Ginny slowly rounded a sloping curve, she noticed a car stuck in a snowdrift at the bottom of the hill.

Dismissing the recollected warnings that floated through her mind about stopping to help strangers, she pulled her car off the road and offered assistance.

"I can't believe you stopped," said the man in the car. "I was afraid I'd be stuck here all night. Maybe if you drive the car while I push it, we can get it out."

The two of them worked at it for nearly forty-five minutes, and sure enough, they managed to get the car out of the drift. Ginny drove it to the top of the hill, then ran back down to get her own car.

"Thank you very much," the anonymous stranger said. "You've been a tremendous help to me." He then reached into her car, grabbed her purse — filled with money and credit cards — and said, "Thanks again. This will do nicely." He ran up the hill, got into his car, and drove away.

Ginny watched in disbelief.

Violated!

If you've ever had anything stolen from you, you know the sudden feelings of frustration and violation which accompany that experience. *How could someone do this to me?* you ask. *What did I do to deserve it? Why me? What audacity!*

Whenever something is stolen or taken from us — whether it's hard-earned money, an irreplaceable keepsake, or an expensive necessity — we feel angry and offended. It's not because we worship what we own, or because we equate our worth with our possessions. It's simply that we have a deep-seated need to protect our personal property rights. We believe that if we agree to leave another person's possessions alone, he should agree to respect our property as well. If he violates that assumed agreement, we feel offended.

And so does God. Despite the ongoing political debate over whether private citizens should own personal property, the Bible apparently assumes that individuals will own a certain amount of their own property. The eighth commandment protects such holdings by absolutely forbidding stealing — which is the *illegitimate* acquisition of property. Thus, before we discuss the varieties of stealing common in our society, it might be beneficial to look at a few *legitimate* means of acquiring property.

Acceptable Means of Acquisition

In his Epistle to the Ephesians, Paul notes, "Let him who steals steal no longer; but rather let him labor, performing with his own hands what is good, in order that he may have something

84

to share with him who has need" (4:28). The first biblically ordained means of acquiring money or property, therefore, is diligent labor.

As much as we might like to find shortcuts that would allow us to avoid work, for most of us, there are none. Whether we're tradesmen or salesmen, teachers or preachers, we all have to do the same thing—work, earn, save, and then with God's direction, purchase earthly goods. But that's not really such an undesirable process, for with it comes a feeling of self-respect. We can enjoy the knowledge that we labored diligently, budgeted wisely, and acquired property to use personally or to give away as God directs.

I remember the first car I ever purchased. I slaved away for a long time and finally saved enough money to buy it—a beauty that was worth every bit of the $425 I paid for it. I couldn't even drive it legally, since I was only fifteen, but I was thrilled. I had the same feeling young couples have when they make the down payment on their first house. I knew I had worked hard, I had saved my money faithfully, and I had made a sensible purchase (in my eyes, anyway!).

The second biblically acceptable means of acquiring property is through sagacious trading, bartering, or investing. In the Parable of the Talents (Matt. 25:14-30), Jesus conveys His approval of the wise investor; likewise, He tells us to "be shrewd as serpents, and innocent as doves" (Matt. 10:16). While the Bible obviously leaves no room for shady business deals or unnecessary gambles, astute investment and barter are acceptable and admirable means of acquiring property.

The third biblical means of acquisition is faithful prayer. From time to time, when people have no opportunities for labor or barter, and every avenue of provision seems closed, God may choose to supply their needs Himself—if they pray. He may provide a piece of property, a given sum of money, or a necessary portion of food—whatever He chooses. And often, such items arrive just in the nick of time.

During the early years of our church ministry, Lynne and I often experienced God's caring provision. When the church

LAWS OF THE HEART

could not support us, He moved individuals to give us everything from cars to food to furniture. When we had no means to help ourselves, God ministered to us through His children.

A Serious Warning!

Any discussion of acquisition is incomplete if it fails to consider the sober question Jesus asked His disciples: "For what will a man be profited, if he gains the whole world, and forfeits his soul? Or what will a man give in exchange for his soul?" (Matt. 16:26)

The Bible says repeatedly that there's more to life than the acquisition of property; if the accumulation of wealth is the primary motivating force in our lives, we're missing the boat. I once heard a speaker remark that he never saw a hearse pulling a U-Haul. And, while said in jest, that simple saying holds a wealth of truth.

Jesus expressed the same thought when He shared the parable of the rich man who tore down his barns and built bigger ones to contain all his wealth. The man viewed his vast treasure and said to himself, "Take your ease, eat, drink, and be merry." But God said to him, "You fool! This very night your soul is required of you; and now who will own what you have prepared?" (Luke 12:16-21) Said Jesus, "So is the man who lays up treasure for himself, and is not rich toward God."

In childhood Sunday School classes, we learn that it is more important to build up treasure in heaven than to amass treasure on earth. But how do we do that? How can we be "rich toward God"? Scripture makes it clear that we store up treasures in heaven each time we use the resources God has given us to accomplish His will in the world. Each time we allow our resources to spill over into other people's lives—when we give to the needy, or support the ministry of the church—we build our account in heaven.

Many men and women have gotten so caught up in the business of "wheeling and dealing" that they've neglected the most important issues of life. Like the rich man in Jesus' parable, their barns overflow, but their souls are empty. Are you one of those people? If you had to strip away the armor of your wealth, who would you be? If you had to stand before God today, what would you have to offer Him? A mind that knows Him? A heart that loves Him? A life that has served Him? Or would God push aside the heaps of clutter you call wealth and find you empty-handed? Would Jesus sadly tell the Father He never knew you?

If you've been so caught up in the business of acquisition that you've neglected your soul, please get off the treadmill long enough to address these eternal issues. Commit yourself to learning who God is, and how you can establish a meaningful relationship with Him.

Perhaps you've already done that. Perhaps you've established a relationship with God through Jesus Christ, and you have the assurance of your eternal salvation. But are you growing as you should be? Are you nurturing your spiritual life? Are you serving God through your involvement in the local church? Or have you gotten so caught up in your career—the building of *your* kingdom—that you have forgotten about the building of *God's* kingdom? Where does your energy go? And your time? Do you have any left to commit to God's work?

The true believer ought to work diligently so he can support himself, his family, and give to others in need. But he ought not be so consumed by his work that he neglects his spiritual life.

The true believer who has been blessed with abundant resources ought to invest and barter intelligently—being as shrewd as a serpent, and as gentle as a dove—but he shouldn't do so simply so he can stockpile his own wealth. Rather, he ought to submit every portion of his wealth to God and seek His direction as to how it should be used.

The true believer who has a legitimate need should pray with faith for God's provision, but he must pray carefully. James tells us that sometimes we ask "with wrong motives, so that [we] may spend it on [our] pleasures" (4:3). We ask as though we had legitimate needs, when we're really just succumbing to materialistic desires. We ask God to hand us things on silver platters, when we really should be working for them.

The Bible assumes we'll each have a certain amount of personal property. And as we've seen, it even mentions acceptable means of acquiring property and provides measures for its protection. Along with the privilege of ownership, however, comes a warning. We must never abuse those legitimate means of acquisition, nor should we allow ourselves to become so consumed by them that we "forfeit our souls."

Shades of Seizure

The eighth commandment acknowledges that some people will *not* confine themselves to legitimate means of acquiring personal property. They will, instead, seek wealth through an illegitimate means — stealing.

The most obvious form of stealing is seizure — or good, old-fashioned theft. An individual decides he wants something that belongs to someone else, so he takes it. He may be motivated by greed, envy, or discontent with what God has entrusted to him. At any rate, he takes matters into his own hands and steals what is not rightly his.

Regrettably, this activity has been going on for centuries. In the Parable of the Good Samaritan (Luke 10:25-37), Jesus told the story of a man traveling from Jerusalem to Jericho. En route to his destination, he was ambushed, beaten, and robbed. Elsewhere in the Gospels, we read that Jesus was crucified between two thieves — common criminals who assaulted people and took their property.

Yes, thievery was common in Jesus' day, as it is in ours. Yet many of us respond to God's prohibition against stealing in the same way we react to His prohibition against murder: "Why waste time on this commandment? I'm no thief. I would never seize another person's possessions. Let's move on."

But I think I can safely say that just as it's possible to murder a man in more than one fashion, it's also possible to steal from him in a variety of ways. There are shades of seizure that seem almost innocent on the surface; but in reality, they fit squarely within the context of theft.

What about employees helping themselves to company supplies without permission — automotive parts, tools, staplers, paper, pencils, pens, notebooks, gasoline, oil, food? Just take a little here and there. It's no big deal. Or is it? Is helping yourself to another person's property a biblical means of acquiring property? You didn't labor for it. You didn't invest, barter, or trade for it. You didn't pray for it. You didn't even ask for it. The fact is, you stole it.

Several retailers I know have said they lose more merchandise through employee theft than through public theft. They fear their allies more than their enemies. They're more paranoid about being ripped off from the inside than from the outside. What does that tell us? It indicates that people in the twentieth century are getting very comfortable with the practice of helping themselves to what is not rightfully theirs.

Another shade of seizure is long-term borrowing. What about the neighbor's ladder you borrowed two years ago? Or that paint brush or punch bowl or serving platter? How about those books, tapes, and albums? You said you'd return them, but did you? Did you truly borrow them? Or did you quietly claim them as yours simply by neglecting to return them?

I challenge you, as I've had to challenge myself, to take out a pencil and paper and make a list of everything in your possession that is not rightfully yours. List everything you've taken from your place of employment, everything you've "borrowed" from the shop, everything you've received on loan from friends and neighbors. Then, make a covenant between yourself and God to return everything on your list to its proper owner by the end of the month.

Maybe you'll have to pack some things up in a UPS box and send them back to their owner. Perhaps you'll have to send a money order to cover the cost of supplies and articles you've already used, lost, or broken. You might want to include a note explaining that you now realize what you did was wrong.

You've decided to honor God and cleanse your conscience by admitting your sin and making restitution.

You could sign your note, "A Convicted Christian," but I think "A Liberated Christian" might be more accurate. Stealing jeopardizes our self-esteem, produces anxiety, and destroys our credibility as Christians. But repentance and restitution free us. They release us from the binding chains of guilt, and allow us to establish peace with ourselves, with others, and with God.

Differing Weights

The second biblically unacceptable way to acquire personal property is through deception, which allows us to steal from others without actually breaking into their homes and running off with their possessions.

Proverbs tells us that "differing weights are an abomination to the Lord, and a false scale is not good" (20:23). Obviously, the practice of doctoring scales is not new. As far back as Old Testament times, men and women were trying to cheat and deceive one another in order to get a little more for their money.

We use a more sophisticated form of "differing weights" today—in the form of smooth-sounding lines. We've all heard them: "Have I got a deal for you—a pretty little piece of land in south central Florida. It'll be a great investment and a perfect retirement spot!" The salesman forgets to mention, however, that this choice piece of real estate is located in the middle of the Everglades.

And how about this one: "I have a mint-condition '78 LeSabre. A little old lady drove it to church once a week and to bridge club when it didn't rain—really! This car was meant for you. It's a steal!" *Sure* it is!

I saw enough of the produce business to know that when a wholesaler says he has 500 cases of lettuce as fresh as the morning dew, you'd better check to make sure the morning dew hasn't gotten a little slimy and brown around the edges!

And what about the realtor who says, "The minute I saw this house, I knew it was the one for you," when he knows the payments will overextend you financially? Or the repairman who insists that your slightly outdated furnace "absolutely must be replaced—immediately"?

I could go on and on. But I'm sure you get the point. Lies, half-truths, schemes, gimmicks, promotions, tricks—they may pass for slick sales pitches, but they're nothing more than sophisticated forms of stealing. Whether they're motivated by greed, envy, or the lust for power, they stand in direct violation of the eighth commandment.

Several years ago a newly divorced woman, with critical financial problems, asked me if the church could give her some temporary financial assistance. We now have a Benevolence Board which handles such requests, offers counseling, and provides financial assistance to legitimately needy people. But at the time, this Board had not yet been established. I suggested, therefore, that she bring her financial records to my office and we'd go over them together. Though the church had very little money to spare, we were willing to help her if we could.

She brought a whole briefcase full of papers into my office, and as I flipped through a stack of rather sizable bills, I noticed one in particular. It was a little, handwritten bill for a tune-up on her car. The cost? Seven hundred dollars.

She explained that her car had been running fine, but some of her co-workers suggested she get a tune-up before winter arrived; "preventative medicine" they called it. She took her car to the suggested dealer and asked for his "winterization special." He had the car for two hours and returned it to her with the bill for $700, which she paid. He didn't give her an itemized receipt. He just told her there was "a lot wrong with it."

I was very angry at that man. He might as well have broken into her home, rummaged through her belongings, and taken $700 in cold cash. Essentially, he did the same thing by deceiving her.

Seizure and deception are very similar in the eyes of God.

They're both forms of stealing. That's why we need to be careful about how we present our information, our products, and our services.

Paul tells us to speak "the truth in love" (Eph. 4:15). That means that sometimes the realtor may have to say, "This is a nice house, and I could see you living in it. But I know your financial condition, and I'm afraid the payments would put you under." The produce salesman would have to say, "I have 500 cases of lettuce, but I'm not sure it's as fresh as you'd like it. Why don't you check through a few cases, see how it looks, and we'll strike a deal." The repairman might have to say, "I don't think you really need a *new* furnace. You could get by with your present one for a few more years."

We may be able to deceive other people, but we can never deceive God. He won't be mocked. He won't be taken in by our clever schemes. What we sow, we also will reap. If we sow dishonesty, we will reap condemnation. But if we sow honesty, integrity, and concern for others, we will reap God's blessing.

Unrighteous Withholdings

The third unacceptable means of acquiring personal property or money is through defrauding—or withholding something from someone to whom it is rightfully due.

Several years ago, my mother loaned $1,000 to a man who had been a friend of my father's. He signed a promissory note, agreeing to repay the money in six months. Six months passed, with no repayment and no request for an extension. Then one year passed, then eighteen months, then two years.

My mother finally called me and suggested that I step in and handle the matter. I said, "Mom, God has blessed us richly. We don't need that money. Maybe the man is really going through hard times. Let's be patient." She agreed and let the matter rest.

Not long thereafter, my mother went out for dinner with some of her friends. However, as she arrived at the restaurant, she saw this man drive up in a brand-new car. He got out, said "Hi" to my mother, and walked into the restaurant.

Mom called me the next day and firmly suggested that I confront the man. "Doesn't the Bible say something about his behavior?" she asked.

Yes, the Bible does say something about that. It calls this type of activity defrauding, and forbids it. When we use our creditors' money for unnecessary goods and services, we are defrauding them by withholding that which is rightfully theirs. If we have an agreed-upon payment plan, and we are on schedule with our payments, then we have the freedom to employ godly discretion in using leftover funds. But if we're behind on payments — and thus not upholding our agreements with various creditors — we are wrong to use their money to acquire property or to "wine and dine" ourselves. We are engaging in just another form of sophisticated stealing.

Many ways exist to defraud people. One method was used in our church parking lot not long ago. A man who had just started attending our church ordered a new car for his wife, but before the car arrived, he was killed in a tragic airplane accident. His widow continued coming to church and showed Lynne and me her new car as soon as it arrived. Naturally, she had strong sentimental ties to the car because it was the last gift her husband had given her.

During one of our church services, someone ran into her new car and did several hundred dollars worth of damage. Naturally, the widow was grieved by the damage done to it, but she was even more hurt by the fact that the person who hit her car failed to acknowledge it. He or she left no explanatory note, no notice to the church office, and no offer to cover expenses.

The man or woman who hit that car is guilty of stealing $300 from a young widow. And in the process, he or she damaged the witness of our church, left our elders with a sticky problem to solve, and laid one more weight on the shoulders of a woman who already was immensely burdened.

Unfortunately, such duplicitous behavior is not unique. It's become quite fashionable to defraud the government by failing to declare certain income, or by taking questionable deductions. It's also a common practice to defraud one's company by calling in sick when we're not, by making personal phone calls when they're forbidden, or by padding expense accounts when we're traveling. Many people even defraud their families by withholding alimony or child support. But these practices, though common, are not acceptable. We have no right to defraud anyone else — whether that means a young widow, a friend or relative, a credit officer, our company, the government . . . or God.

In Malachi, God accuses the people of Israel of robbing Him. When they ask how they have robbed Him, He replies, "In tithes and contributions" (3:8). The principle of the tithe is taught throughout the Old Testament and is mentioned twice by Jesus. It tells us that 10 percent of everything we earn should be given back to God through the administration of the local church. But the Israelites were not doing that. They were keeping the tithe for themselves, and defrauding God of what was rightfully His.

Many Christians today do the same thing. They let greed, self-centeredness, and materialism keep them from obeying God. They use their tithe for personal desires — extra clothes, entertainment, furniture, pleasure, and a host of other nonessentials — rather than for the work of the kingdom. Like the Israelites before them, they rob the God who has given them all they have.

The eighth commandment boldly declares that we should acquire property only through biblically acceptable means. We should work diligently, invest wisely, and pray in faith with pure motives. We should never seize what belongs to another person, never deceive another person, and never defraud another person — including God. This commandment offers a stiff challenge in regard to our means of doing business and acquiring property. But it also offers a generous reward — a clean conscience and a sense of liberation that allows us to enjoy fully the property and possessions God has enabled us to acquire. Try it. You'll see!

Hold to the Truth

"You shall not bear false witness against your neighbor"
(Exodus 20:16).

Once upon a time, in a faraway land, a church was born — and
oh, what a church it was! It had the usual singing, preaching,
and giving. But it also had much, much more: intense, all-night
praying, bold and effective witnessing, and selfless, God-glorifying sharing. Rumor had it that the people in this church shared
their resources so freely, that poverty actually had vanished
from among its members. And the little church grew and grew.

In fact, it grew so fast that soon the Sunday morning offerings
were not sufficient to meet the needs of all the poor people
who were adding their names to the membership rolls. What
was the growing church to do? They called a meeting. One man
suggested they sponsor bingo games. Another suggested a char-
iot wash. Yet another suggested a church bazaar and bake sale.

Suddenly, one man jumped to his feet and said excitedly,
"Hey, I've got a great idea! I have a little summer cottage down
by the seashore. I can sell it and give the profits to our needy
church brothers." Everyone cheered and clapped. Another man
stood up and said, "Say, I have an empty lot over by Elm and

Vine. I can sell that and do the same thing." Another round of cheering and applause erupted.

So began one of the most exciting eras the little church had ever enjoyed. Whenever a need could not be met through the regular Sunday offering, someone would sell something and bring the profits to the church leaders; they, in turn, would distribute the money to those with legitimate needs. God continued to bless that church, and it continued to grow.

Then one day a curious thing happened. Several needy people had just joined the church, and as usual, someone volunteered to sell a piece of land and donate the proceeds. But when the donor handed the money bag over to the pastor, the pastor started shouting at him. Bewildered bystanders listened to his angry words. "Why have you done this awful thing? You have not just lied to men. You have lied to God!" Immediately, the man fell down dead. The congregation gasped, while the pastor calmly turned around and ordered some young men to carry the body out and bury it.

The pastor then explained that the man did indeed sell his property. But instead of giving the full amount to the church, he and his wife had decided to keep some money for themselves. That, however, wasn't the crux of their problem. Their *real* problem lay in the fact that they led other church members to believe they were donating the full amount. They wanted to impress people and make them think they were as generous and godly as others had been. In reality, they were selfish liars.

At that moment, the wife of the deceased man wandered into the crowd, unaware of what had just happened. The hushed crowd listened intensely as the pastor looked her straight in the eyes and held out the familiar money bag. "Does this contain the full amount that you received for the land?" he asked. Everyone in the room held their breath. Their hearts pounded wildly, their palms perspired, and they silently pleaded, *Say no! Say no! Tell the truth. Don't lie!*

The wife looked at the pastor calmly, and said, "Yes, of course, that's the full amount. That's what we promised, isn't it?"

The pastor shook his head sadly. "You are not just lying to me, you know. You also are lying to God. The footsteps you hear are the footsteps of those who buried your husband. Now they are coming for you." Immediately she fell down dead, and the men buried her beside her husband.

That day, the members of that little church agreed that it was in their best interest to tell the truth, the whole truth, and nothing but the truth.

God Is Truth

You probably recognized this paraphrased treatment of the story of Ananias and Sapphira (Acts 5:1-10). It's a true, historical account of what happened in the early church at Jerusalem when two members of the church decided to lie.

Most of us, like Ananias and Sapphira, have no idea how intensely God hates dishonesty and how angry it makes Him. But we really shouldn't be surprised by God's reaction to dishonesty. We read in Scripture that truth is bound up in the very identity of God. Pontius Pilate was neither the first nor the last to ask, "What is truth?" But to him, and every other seeker, Jesus gives the final answer when He says, "*I* am the way, and the *truth*, and the life" (John 14:6; italics mine).

"Don't gaze wistfully into space," we can almost hear Jesus say. "You won't find truth there. Nor will you find it deep within yourself. You'll only find truth in Me, for I am God, and God is Truth."

If God is Truth, then untruth—or dishonesty—is the antithesis of His being. It is contrary to His essence, and therefore utterly disgusting to Him. Falsehood cannot be tolerated by one who is intrinsically truthful.

Imagine an accomplished pianist—someone with perfect pitch—who is asked to perform on a piano that is woefully out of tune. Could he tolerate the grating disharmony for long? Or think of a skilled tradesman who views a poorly constructed building. Would uneven walls and unmatched trim bother him?

Or put yourself in the place of a competent driver who is forced to "give the wheel" to a rookie. Could you sit back and quietly ignore the inexperienced driver's reckless techniques? Of course not! You couldn't tolerate that anymore than the pianist could tolerate the discordant piano, or the tradesman the shoddy workmanship. How then, can we possibly expect the God of Truth to tolerate dishonesty?

We read in Proverbs that there are seven things which God hates: "Haughty eyes, a lying tongue, and hands that shed innocent blood, a heart that devises wicked plans, feet that run rapidly to evil, a false witness who utters lies, and one who spreads strife among brothers" (6:16-19). Two of these seven "abominations to Him" have to do with verbal dishonesty. It is to these sins that the ninth commandment speaks.

In the remaining pages of this chapter we will look at three ways to speak dishonestly or give false witness — lying, distortion, and exaggeration.

From the Father of Lies

On any given night, one can pick up a newspaper and read scathing accounts of human atrocities — the assassination of world leaders, terrorist warfare, child abuse, political corruption, drug-related violence, rape, murder. The list goes on and on and we ask, "Where will it all end?" Perhaps a better question might be, "Where did it all begin?"

Scripture tells us that the cesspool of evil which has flooded our planet began with a lie. When God placed Adam and Eve in the Garden of Eden He told them not to eat of one particular tree: "For in the day that you eat from it you shall surely die" (Gen. 2:17). But along came the serpent, "who was more crafty than any beast of the field which the Lord God had made"; and he said, "You surely shall not die! For God knows that in the day you eat from it your eyes will be opened, and you will be like God, knowing good and evil" (Gen. 3:1, 4-5). You know the rest of the story.

Jesus called Satan the "father of lies" (John 8:44), and through the serpent, Satan affirmed that identity. While God is by nature truthful, Satan is an inveterate liar. With his lie to Eve, he opened the floodgates of sin. Since then, he's been busy whispering lies into the hearts and minds of all God's children.

Many of us get caught up in lies — so caught up that we begin to adopt Satan's role. In theory we align ourselves with the God of truth, but in practice we wear the hat of a liar. Why do we do it?

Sometimes we lie to impress people. We claim to be bosom buddies with important people we barely know to boost our status. We lie when we fill out job applications to assure ourselves a position. We lie about past accomplishments to win acclaim.

Sometimes we lie to get revenge. We're angry with someone, so we make up stories to discredit them. Sometimes we lie to make a profit, as we discussed in the previous chapter. At other times we lie for convenience. We make excuses for not lending assistance to someone, when really, we simply don't want to get involved. We say we'll come to a party, when we have no intention of doing so. We just don't have the courage to say no.

At other times, we lie to escape punishment. I probably could fill a book with the lies people tell policemen to avoid getting traffic tickets. And what parent doesn't have a long list of "logical explanations" they've heard from a son or daughter who's missed curfew? Professors too spend untold hours listening to heartrending (though untrue) stories of why an assignment wasn't turned in on time.

Yes, we lie to impress, to get revenge, to make a profit, for convenience, and to escape punishment. In short, we lie a lot! That's why Paul had to tell us to lay aside falsehood, and "speak truth" (Eph. 4:25). How we'd love to claim textual ambiguity in regard to this verse. *What is Paul really trying to say?* we'd like to ask. *What is his hidden meaning?* Yet as hard as we try to escape its implications, this verse stares us in the face and jars us with its simplicity. *"Stop lying!"* Paul said. *"Start telling the truth!"*

Nothing destroys the personal credibility of a Christian like a lying tongue. Have you ever heard someone say, "Well, yes, I know that's what he *said*, but you know him. You can't believe a thing he tells you." Or, "I know she *claimed* to be the winner, but she's never been known for truthfulness." Or, "Why should I believe what you say about God? I can't believe anything *else* you say." Christians who lie might as well accept the fact that they can't be effective examples or spokesmen for Christ. We can't honor the God of truth with a mouth that spews forth lies.

We live in a society that minimizes the seriousness of lying. We've been conditioned to accept dishonesty with a sigh and a shrug of the shoulders. That's why it's so hard to break the behavioral pattern of lying.

The only sure way to snap this pattern is to declare all-out spiritual war. Everytime the Holy Spirit convicts us about lying, we have to go right back to the person to whom we've lied and say, "I hate to admit this, but I lied to you. I didn't tell you the truth."

If you've ever done that, you know how humiliating the experience is. And you know that after doing it two or three times, you're going to think long and hard before you tell another lie.

Those of us who are parents must confront dishonesty whenever we detect it in our children. The sooner we disrupt the pattern, the easier it will be to break. I've had some long talks with my kids about lying—like the time neither of them would admit spilling apple juice on the new carpet, and the time my daughter said she didn't have any homework when she really did, and the time my son claimed to know nothing about the greasy smear on the wall, and the time. . . .

The end of our conversations usually goes something like this: "Hey, kids, spilling a little apple juice is not the end of the world. I won't condemn you for life because you had an accident. I'll just ask you to clean it up. No big deal. But when you lie to me, that's another story. Lying is serious business! God can't tolerate it, and neither can I. He'll forgive you for it, and so will I. But we can only forgive you if you admit it. So go to your room and think about it. We all make mistakes, but we should never lie about them."

Now and then I have to give myself the same little pep talk I give my kids. I'm as prone to hedge the truth as they are—and as you are. Will you join me in waging war against the father of lies? Can we commit ourselves to honoring the God of truth?

Quote—Unquote

Distortion is a subtle form of lying. When we distort something, we don't utter bold-faced lies; we simply twist the truth.

One of the most common forms of distortion is misquoting. For politicians, movie stars, and other prominent personalities, being misquoted is a constant source of frustration. A player from the Chicago Bears recently told me how angry he got when he read the sports page version of an interview he had given. His statements were misquoted and taken out of context; the resulting impression was that he was very critical of both the coaching staff and other players on the team. This player was a Christian and had diligently been trying to build bridges with other team members. Naturally, the distorted comments thwarted his efforts.

It's so easy to destroy someone's reputation by distorting their words. I've had people enter my office who were outraged over something I allegedly had said. Time and time again I've had to defend myself against misquotes. On occasion, I've even had to play a tape of a given message to prove I didn't say what I was reported to have said! And once, during a fund raiser, I publicly announced that an anonymous donor had promised to match whatever sum of money we raised, up to $500,000. A rumor then began circulating in our community that an anonymous "Korean donor" had given our church a large sum of money; this was an obvious indication that we were tied in with the "Moonies." You can see how ridiculous—and harmful—this distortion was. Not only were words put in my mouth, but conclusions were carelessly and erroneously drawn.

We distort the words of public personalities, neighbors, bosses, employees, friends, spouses, and even God. In Galatians, Paul warns about those who "want to distort the Gospel of Christ" (1:7). It's one thing to distort the words of other human beings, but quite another to distort the words of God. Paul firmly says that individuals who do such a thing should "be accursed" (Gal. 1:8). Yet it *does* happen, repeatedly, when men and women mishandle truth. Mormons, Jehovah's Witnesses, Moonies — and a host of others — twist the Scriptures to prove their points. They put together a mixture of truth, half-truth, and non-truth, and come up with their particular brand of religion.

But it's not only cultists who distort Scripture. Some Christians also twist the Word of God to suit their own ends. In some parts of this country, Christians defend racism from a supposedly biblical base. They defend segregation policies with the same Book that says, "There is neither Jew nor Greek, there is neither slave nor free man, there is neither male nor female; for you are all one in Christ Jesus" (Gal. 3:28).

Others use Jesus' own words to defend oppression policies. They claim that Jesus' statement, "the poor you have with you always" (Matt. 26:11), frees us from our responsibility to care for the needy and disadvantaged. They take one verse out of context and use it to nullify everything else that Jesus, and the whole of Scripture, says about the poor.

Whether we're using the words of other people, or the phrases of Scripture, we have to make every effort to use those words carefully and accurately. Misquoting and taking words out of context, are nothing more than subtle lies.

The Superlative Syndrome

Exaggeration is the most problematic area of truthfulness for me, because I find it so easy to slip into the "superlative syndrome." When I read a book I appreciate, I want to tell everyone that it's "absolutely great." If I see a movie that's not all it was cracked up to be, I want to make sure everyone knows "it stinks." But sometimes I present the object of my analysis in a better or worse light than it appeared in reality.

And why not? Exaggeration is the basis upon which many of our most common colloquialisms are built. On a nice day, we say, "There's not a cloud in the sky." On a rainy day, we say, "It's raining buckets." When we see an attractive girl, we say, "She's a knockout." When we injure ourselves, we say, "Boy, I almost killed myself." But how many times have you seen a truly cloudless day? Or buckets fall from the sky? Or a girl who literally "knocks people out" with her beauty? And how many times have you truly been close to death?

Have you ever heard a sports commentator say, "So-and-so is the best wide receiver in the NFL"? I've heard it many times, and I've always been amused when I hear the same commentator make the same statement the following week — about a different player! Johnny Carson does something similar when he introduces guests on "The Tonight Show." It seems that everyone on his show is "the best." Of course, it's not too hard to be the best in a superlative society.

Exaggeration usually is harmless, but it can be dangerous when it's used destructively. A husband sits in a counselor's office and says, "My wife *never* wants to attend important business functions with me." The wife says, "Well, you *always* humiliate me in public." The husband says, "You *never* express interest in my needs." The wife says, "You're *always* too busy to pay attention to me." Exaggeration polarizes a conversation and prohibits constructive communication.

Exaggeration even goes on in Christian circles. The music department at our church has a hard time selecting songs and choruses to use because so many of them exaggerate the truth. They present the Christian life as a bed of roses, filled with unending peace and happiness. They give the impression that Christians are somehow insulated from tragedy and disappoint-ment, from problems and hardship. And that's a lie, a lie that unbelievers see through immediately.

Subtle lies like that even crop up now and then in testimonies. The young man who smoked an occasional joint in his pre-Christian days now claims he had a $400-a-day drug habit. Of course he's stretching the truth, but what a dramatic testimony of deliverance it makes! Or a woman confesses that before she became a Christian, she was lonely, empty, joyless, and insecure. But when she met Christ, He solved *all* her problems. Now she feels His presence *all* the time, is *constantly* filled with joy, and has the confidence to accomplish *great* things. God just keeps blessing and blessing!

Yes, God *does* keep blessing, but we lose our integrity as Christians when we overstate those blessings and portray a paradise that doesn't exist.

Fund raising is another art that appears to benefit from the practice of exaggeration. Christian television personalities have been known to exaggerate their financial needs in order to move the masses. "This will be our last show," they cry, "unless you respond. Our bills must be paid within one week. If they're not, we're going off the air. It all depends on you." Sometimes, of course, such claims are legitimate; but in other instances, financial statements have proven them false. Organizations have pleaded financial despair when, in fact, they had millions of dollars in excess funds. How that must grieve the heart of God. Christian organizations have a duty to represent their financial standings honestly.

Every year we hire professional auditors from a "Big Eight" firm to do a certified audit of our church finances. We want to be able to present our entire financial picture to anyone who has a question. When we have a need, we present it openly. When the need is met, we say it's been met. When we have unexpected expenses or revenues, we explain how we handled the deficit or the excess. This is our way of avoiding exaggeration and distortion in the financial realm.

James tells us to "let [our] yes be yes, and [our] no, no" (5:12). Instead of getting all caught up in superlatives, we ought to take his advice and stick to the unblemished truth. We ought to speak in such a way that others can take our words at face value, confident that they accurately and objectively represent the truth.

Know the Truth

It's vitally important that we handle *truths* properly. It's also crucial that we handle *Truth*—the ultimate Truth of the Gospel—properly. But before we can treat it properly, we have to *know* it. Every Sunday morning I look up and down the rows in our church auditorium and see people who enjoy a variety of relationships with Truth. Some have heard Truth and responded to it. Others have heard it, but haven't yet decided how to respond. Others have never heard it.

Perhaps some of you who are reading this book fit into that third category. You have never heard the Truth of the Gospel of Jesus Christ. For that reason, I would like to present it here, in the form of four great truths that we all should know.

The first truth is that we all are moral failures. That's not my opinion, or even the opinion of the early church fathers. It's a truth established by God Himself (Rom. 3:23). And it's a truth we have to come to grips with personally. Satan whispers many lies to the contrary—but the fact remains. No matter how "good" we appear in comparison to other people, we all fall dismally short of God's perfect moral standards.

As I mentioned in an earlier chapter, the summary of the Law is given in Mark's Gospel: "Hear, O Israel; the Lord our God is one Lord; and you shall love the Lord your God with all your heart, and with all your soul, and with all your mind, and with all your strength. . . . You shall love your neighbor as yourself" (12:29-31). After reading those words this morning, I had to get down on my knees and confess to God that I don't love Him the way I should. Nor do I obey His Word the way I ought to.

Why did I have to confess that? Because it's the truth about who I am. I am a sinful man who loves in bits and pieces and gives a halfhearted response to the One who loves me purely. I can't hide that truth from God. And I can't respond to the Truth of the Gospel until I get honest about myself—and about my sin.

The second great truth is that someday we're going to stand in the blazing brilliance of God's holiness. Then all our shams and cover-ups will be seen for what they really are. Every little sin will stand out like a hideous stain. We may be able to hide the truth about ourselves now, but there'll come a day when the condition of our souls will be painfully evident.

The third great truth is that people who have not repented will be doomed to an eternity in hell. Again, that's not my idea. And I wish I didn't have to talk about it. But the Bible says it's true. Unrepentant sinners will be separated from God forever and dwell in a place where evil will be unleashed in its full, unrestrained horror (Rev. 20:15).

The fourth great truth is that those who admit their sinfulness, and ask Jesus Christ to forgive them and become their Lord and Savior, will escape the judgment of hell and enter the kingdom of heaven.

Satan, of course, doesn't like to hear Truth. So he counters every word of Truth with a lie. "Don't worry," he says. "The pastor's just revved up. He doesn't know what he's talking about. You have good intentions, don't you? That's all you need. Take it easy. It'll all come out in the wash. God'll be easy on you!"

Those are lies—smooth sounding ones, maybe—but lies, nonetheless. Satan told Eve that she would become like God. Did she? He also said she'd never die. Did she?

The Bible says we have to admit the truth about ourselves—that we're sinners. Then we have to repent of our sin and reach out for the mercy and grace of Jesus Christ. That is our only hope.

Have you done that? Have you been honest about your sin? Have you asked Jesus Christ to forgive you? If you have, then you can rest in the promise of eternal life. If you haven't, please give careful thought to the Gospel of Truth. And then respond.

Ten
Crave Contentment

"You shall not covet your neighbor's house; you shall not covet your neighbor's wife or his male servant or his female servant or his ox or his donkey or anything that belongs to your neighbor" (Exodus 20:17).

When I was growing up, I greatly appreciated the fact that my father went out of his way to commend me for being a responsible, levelheaded kid. By the time I was a junior in high school, I had my private pilot's license and my dad granted me free access to his produce company's planes. During the summer, he allowed me to use his forty-five foot sailboat. When I worked at the company farms, he entrusted me with the largest and most expensive farm equipment. He even had the dockhands teach me to drive huge tractor-trailer rigs, and he let me drive them to Florida to pick up loads of produce.

In his eyes, I was seventeen going on thirty-seven. He trusted me, he expressed that trust often, and I valued it more than anything else in the world.

But one day I did something that threatened the very fiber of that trust. I told him I wanted to buy a motorcycle.

"A *motorcycle?*" he asked in disbelief. "Why do you want a

motorcycle? They're totally impractical. You can't haul anything with them, you can't ride them in the rain, and they're dangerous. This is the worst idea you've ever come up with!

"But," he continued, "it's your life. If you've thought this through, and you're sure you want to make a stupid decision that will reflect poorly on your judgment, disappoint me, and break your mother's heart—then go ahead and do it. The decision's yours. I won't try to sway your thinking!"

I thought about what he said for about thirty seconds. Then I called a friend who had a motorcycle for sale; I told him I'd buy it. It was old, slow, noisy, and smoked like a chimney—but I loved it! I was in my glory.

After many months, I finally talked my dad into taking it out for a ride. I stood at the bottom of the driveway and explained the mechanisms to him. He got on, took off like a veteran, and didn't return for an hour. As he put the bike back in the garage, he grudgingly admitted that he had more fun with it than he thought he would.

Not long after, I left for my freshman year in college. When I came home for Thanksgiving break I received the shock of my life. In the garage was a brand-new red, white, and blue 1,200 CC Harley-Davidson. I had never seen anything so magnificent in my life.

Just then my dad walked into the garage sporting a black leather jacket, Harley gloves, and a red, white, and blue helmet. "Let's go riding," he said. "Who cares if it's snowing!"

Later that night—as we were thawing out—he told me he had been in Chicago buying produce when he saw a 1,200 CC bike in the window of a Harley dealer. He stopped in to look it over, and all of a sudden, something snapped inside him. He decided he "just had to have that bike!"

He went into the store and made an offer, but the clerk explained that it was the only 1,200 CC available and another man already had placed a deposit on it. The clerk even refused to accept my dad's offer of "cash on the spot." He did say, though, that if the other man didn't pick up the bike the following morning, Dad could buy it.

After a restless night, my dad returned to the store. He was thrilled to see the bike still in the window—until the man in front of him claimed it and handed over his check. While the dealer went into a back room to stamp the man's check, my dad offered the bike's new owner $200 more than he had just paid for it. The man refused to deal.

Disappointed and a little angry, Dad climbed into his truck and headed back home to Kalamazoo. On the way, he came up with an idea. Instead of checking in at the produce company, he went straight to the nearest Harley dealer, found a cycle identical to the one he had seen in Chicago, and bought it. He said he had never been so excited about anything in his life.

In order to appreciate his excitement, and realize how out-of-character this behavior was for my dad, you'd have to know something about his typical attitude toward material possessions. Every year he bought a new car, put 40,000 miles on it without changing the oil or having it serviced, and then traded it back to the Ford dealer for a new one.

Every year the Ford dealer would say, "Well, Harold, can I talk you into some options this year?"

"Just a heater," Dad would say.

"Well, what about a color?" the dealer would ask.

"Cheap," Dad would answer. "Any color that's cheap. I like cheap colors."

Even Dad's wardrobe reflected his indifference to the material world. For one ten-year stretch, he wore nothing but black slacks and white shirts. And he bought his shoes by the case— all the same style and the same color. When people joked about it, he'd say, "It's one less decision I have to make. I reach into the closet and take the end shirt and the end pair of pants. No muss. No fuss. That's the way I like it."

He was so disciplined, so disinterested in frills, so hard to excite—except when it came to Harley-Davidsons. Within two years we had six of them in the garage—two big ones for Dad, one each for my brother and me, and models for my sisters.

One time a close friend of Dad's asked him if he could borrow his Harley to take on a short trip. Dad had a reputation for being generous with what he owned, so this man—a competent biker—didn't anticipate any problems. However, an uncomfortable silence met his request.

Finally Dad said, "You can sleep in my house, you can drive my car, you can sail my boat, you can fly my plane—but please, *please* don't ask to use my Harley!"

The Passion to Possess

Why did I bother to tell you that whole story? Because I think most of us are a little like my dad. We have a weak spot. Whether it's a motorcycle, a home, a boat, clothes, books, stamps, jewelry, furniture, art, music, horses, etc., most of us have a weakness that occasionally gives way to runaway desires. I don't think I've ever met anyone who doesn't have to struggle now and then to control their passion to possess something.

The tenth commandment warns us about this passion to possess. It tells us to be very careful about inordinate desires that encourage us to covet.

Coveting is an all-encompassing compulsion to possess something. It's not merely the act of admiring something. We certainly can appreciate an object for its beauty, workmanship, or function—and express that appreciation freely—without coveting it. But there's a big difference between saying, "I like that," and saying, "I *have* to own it." When we covet something we decide we're not going to rest until we get it.

In the remainder of this chapter, I want to discuss three concepts associated with the tenth commandment—coveting-at-large, coveting that which is your neighbor's, and the art of contentment.

I Want It All!

Never in the history of civilization have people been as "pushed to possess" as we are. Marketing research is a billion-dollar-a-year business. Thousands of people in this country spend forty hours a week designing ways to trigger our buying mechanisms. They use music, slogans, sights, sounds, and colors to inflame our passion to possess. Often they attempt to stimulate fear, nostalgia, pride, sexual arousal, jealousy, or some other intense emotion. Their ultimate goal, though, is to impair our self-control just long enough for us to decide that we simply "must have" their product. They're trying to make us covet.

Advertisers are not, however, the only ones guilty of this ploy. Managers sometimes dangle attractive inducements in front of producers or salesmen in an effort to increase their output. "Just think," they say, "about that Caribbean cruise. Or that golfing vacation in Pebble Beach. Or that huge bonus." Some sales organizations even encourage people to hang color pictures of their dream possessions on their refrigerator, bulletin board, or bathroom mirror. Hopefully, these constant reminders will motivate them to sell more products.

Obviously, not all incentive programs are bad. But when their underlying motivation is to produce a fixation that causes an employee to sacrifice greater values for the sake of profits, those incentives are wrong. Any program, ploy, or advertisement that knowingly creates the climate for covetousness is a tool Satan can use to distract us from spiritual concerns.

Paul says, "If then you have been raised up with Christ, keep seeking the things above, where Christ is, seated at the right hand of God. Set your mind on the things above, not on the things that are on the earth" (Col. 3:1-2). *The Living Bible* says that if we really know the Lord we should "have as little desire for this world as a dead person does" (Col. 3:3, TLB). A familiar chorus tells us that if we "turn our eyes upon Jesus," the things of this world "will grow strangely dim."

Those concepts make sense to me. It seems reasonable to expect that those of us who truly know Christ as Lord and have our attention focused on Him, should have a somewhat detached attitude toward material things. We should realize that though they're a necessary part of our earthly existence, they're not an ultimate value.

111

Why should we, who have been born again to spiritual life, allow ourselves to be controlled by runaway desires? Why should we fix our minds on things that will rust, rot, and depreciate? We are men and women created in the image of God; we've been called to be agents of reconciliation. We're created to accomplish eternal goals. When we fix our minds on transitory commodities and temporal goals, however, we live beneath our privilege.

Therefore, we ought to fix our minds on Jesus and the things that are important to Him. We ought to dream about people, not possessions, and design ways to help them hear the message of God's love. We ought to hang pictures of hungry kids on our refrigerators, names of those for whom we're praying on our bulletin boards, and Scripture verses on our bathroom mirrors.

Last week I borrowed a pickup truck from a staff member of our church. Taped above the fuel gauge were five reasons to worship God. *Those* are the kinds of thoughts that ought to be filling our minds, rather than thoughts about all the "things" we would like to acquire.

Just as coveting-at-large captivates our minds, so it tends to sabotage our convictions. It's not uncommon for us to violate important biblical imperatives in our efforts to acquire the objects of our passion. Sometimes we pursue our passions to the point that our health suffers. Or we neglect our spouses and families. Or we abuse other people for the sake of our selfish ends. Sometimes we even lie and cheat to get what we want.

Those whose convictions have been sabotaged will begin to neglect their relationship with the Lord. They'll forget to pray and read the Bible. They'll have no time for service or ministry. And, of course, they'll be unable to offer financial support to the church or the needy—all their resources will be tied to their passion to possess.

Do you see now why we're living in a dangerous age? Covetousness can so captivate our minds and sabotage our convictions that we are no longer free to love God or be His agents of help to a needy world.

I Want Yours!

The passion to possess is an ugly sin no matter how we look at it. But when the object of our passion belongs to some one else — as the tenth commandment says, "to our neighbor" — this sin takes on an even uglier hue.

When we covet something "out there," something that is available and waiting to be claimed, we limit most of our destruction to ourselves. But when we covet what belongs to others, we bring those people into the situation, and jeopardize our attitudes toward them and our relationships with them.

In high school, I played basketball — not well, mind you, but very enthusiastically. I remember sitting on the bench, consciously wishing that our starting guard would get hurt so I could play. You probably can imagine what kind of relationship I had with that guy. I was envious of his abilities and his opportunities. Everytime I looked at him, one thought went through my mind: *I want your position!*

Have you ever coveted another individual's job? Have you ever found yourself wishing that that person would miss an important deadline, or lose an account, so you could claim his position? Have you ever found yourself trying to make life miserable for him, or trying to sap his energy with inordinate demands? In other words, have you ever let the process of "wishing" for someone else's job push you into the process of "scheming" for it?

Have you ever coveted someone else's spouse? Have you ever made subtle plays for that person? Have you ever berated your own mate and fed your discontent by making insensitive comparisons? Have you ever taken covert action to undermine the solidity of a friend's marriage?

Have you ever heard selfish siblings count the days until a parent dies and frees up the inheritance? Have you ever seen them threaten their aging parents' dignity by making it clear that they value them only for the bank account they've promised to leave?

Coveting what belongs to another person is a serious offense on two counts. First, it indicates our lack of love for our neighbor, our relative, our friend, or whoever owns what we desire. When we place our affections on an inheritance, we remove our love from the person who's bequeathing it to us. When we see our neighbor's wife as the object of our desire, we begin to view our neighbor as the object of our disdain. When we scheme to get someone else's job, we reveal our calloused, insensitive heart. When we wish another person illness, injury, or bad fortune, we make it clear that the only person we care about is "number one"—ourselves. When we covet what belongs to someone else, we displace the owner. In our minds, we kick him out of the game, or out of the job, or out of the marriage.

Coveting another person's possessions also is serious because it unmasks our dissatisfaction with God's provision for us. In our hearts we say, "God, you've not been fair with me. I deserve a nicer wife, or a more lucrative position, or a bigger house, or higher status. You've shortchanged me. You owe me something better!" While we probably wouldn't verbalize those ideas, and may not even be consciously aware of them, they underlie every covetous thought, word, and action. They are, in fact, the basis of the covetous life.

I Have Learned . . .

There is, however, an alternative to the covetous life—the contented life.

Oh, sure, you think, *that's just what I want—to live like a lazy cow who lies on her belly and chews her cud. No action. No ambition. No drive. Sure. Let the world go by without me. I'm contented!*

This may be a realistic description of the proverbial "contented cow," but it has nothing to do with an accurate picture of the contented lifestyle. Contentment is not passive. It's not the absence of ambition. And it's certainly not synonymous with laziness. It's simply a condition of the heart.

One can be relatively poor and be contented. One can be very rich and be contented. And one can fall somewhere in between and be contented. Paul puts it like this:

> Not that I speak from want; for I have learned to be content in whatever circumstances I am. I know how to get along with humble means, and I also know how to live in prosperity; in any and every circumstance I have learned the secret of being filled and going hungry, both of having abundance and suffering need (Phil. 4:11-12).

Contentment is a far cry from the covetous life. Unlike the covetous man who thinks God has dealt him an unfair hand, the contented man is grateful to God for whatever he has. He worships Him whether he's been blessed with little or with much. The contented man knows that if he has Christ as his Lord and Savior, he has everything he needs—and far more than he deserves.

I have only to flip back through the pages of this book to find out what I deserve. I've broken every one of the Ten Commandments to some degree, and because of that, I deserve the full measure of God's wrath. That's what I deserve. That, and nothing else.

But what has God given me? He's given me health, home, family, and friends. He's given me forgiveness, salvation, and the promise of life eternal. He's given me a ministry. He's given me His day-in and day-out presence. How dare I ask for more?

I ought to be asking myself why I have even *that* much. In view of who I am and how I've violated God, why has He blessed me with anything? The answer to that question is that we have a gracious God. He specializes in giving His children far more than they deserve.

When we're tempted to shake our fists at Him and say, "Why did You bless Harry more than You blessed me?" we'd better stop and repent. We'd better admit to God that we're sinful men and women who forget to be grateful. Then we should ask

Him to supernaturally purge the covetous spirit from our hearts.

Job said, "Naked I came from my mother's womb, and naked I shall return there. The Lord gave and the Lord has taken away. Blessed be the name of the Lord" (Job 1:21). Job was able to worship God even when everything he owned and everyone he loved was taken from him. Why? Because he handled everything God gave him with *open hands*. When God blessed him with prosperity, he accepted it with gratitude; but he held it loosely—with open hands. That way, when God chose to repossess it, he could willingly let go.

True believers who want to live the contented life must learn to handle their possessions as Job did. We ought to say, "Thank You, Lord, for this house, and this car, and this job, and my ability to earn. I appreciate all You have done for me and I accept it with a grateful heart. But I hold it loosely, Lord. If You should ever decide that I'd be better off without it, or if You want it to go to someone else, then take it back or reassign it."

A covetous man always wants more. When he gets it, he clutches it with closed fists—and lives in bondage to the fear that he might lose it. The contented man is satisfied with what he has. If God blesses him with more, he receives it graciously, but always is willing to let it go. Because of that, he lives in freedom.

The contented man not only has open hands, but *open arms*—arms that can embrace a brother and rejoice in his good fortune. Imagine that your friend buys a new house, or your neighbor remodels his kitchen, or your co-worker gets a promotion, or your brother-in-law hits it big with a shrewd investment. If you're a covetous man, you'll be filled with envy and anger. You won't be able to rejoice over another person's good fortune. If you're a contented man, you'll say to your friend, "I sure hope you enjoy your new home!" And to your neighbor, "Hey, your new kitchen looks great!" And to your coworker, "Best of luck in your new position!" And to your brother-in-law, "How exciting! I'm thrilled for you!"

The contented man is free to rejoice when another gains— and to weep when another loses. Paul said, "And if one member suffers, all the members suffer with it; if one member is honored, all the members rejoice with it" (1 Cor. 12:26). When the basketball star whose position you want to play gets injured, do you rejoice in your "lucky break" or do you try to feel the anguish of his disappointment? When an acquaintance loses his business, do you gloat over your "good management skills," or do you try to think of ways to help him? Do you laugh at the man who weeps, or do you weep with him?

The covetous man dreams of taking. The contented man dreams of sharing. The covetous man clutches all he has with a tight fist, in fear of others. The contented man holds what he has with open hands, and reaches out to embrace others.

Oh, that we would all learn the joy of the contented life. We're physical, material beings, so we'll always have physical, material needs. But those of us who keep those needs in perspective, who fix our minds on Jesus Christ, and who accept His gifts with grateful hearts, can experience the joy of the contented life.

Laws That Liberate

Paul tells us that "the Law has become our tutor to lead us to Christ, that we may be justified by faith" (Gal. 3:24). In other words, the Law points out our sin, so that we can see our need for a Savior. If reading this book has been a difficult and frustrating experience for you, it may be that the Law has succeeded in doing exactly what it's supposed to do—it's forced you down on your knees in humble repentance.

If that's been true for you, don't hesitate. Jesus is only a prayer away. If you repent of your sin right now, He'll forgive you, enter your life, and begin a good work in you that will continue for the rest of your life. His Holy Spirit will so transform you that in a few years, you'll look back and say, "I'm a different person than I used to be. I still violate God's laws now and then, but I know I'm heading in the right direction. I'm changing. I'm growing. And I'm liberated at last!"

Personal and Group Study Guide

For Personal Study

Settle into your favorite chair with your Bible, a pen or pencil, and this book. Read a chapter, marking portions that seem significant to you. Write in the margins. Note where you agree, disagree, or question the author. Look up footnotes and relevant Scripture passages. Then turn to the questions listed in this study guide. If you want to trace your progress with a written record, use a notebook to record your answers, thoughts, feelings, and further questions. Refer to the text and to the Scriptures as you allow the questions to enlarge your thinking. And pray. Ask God to give you a discerning mind for truth, an active concern for others, and a greater love for Himself.

For Group Study

Plan ahead. Before meeting with your group, read and mark the chapter as if you were preparing for personal study. Glance through the questions making mental notes of how you might contribute to your group's discussion. Bring a Bible and the text to your meeting.

Arrange an environment that promotes discussion. Comfortable chairs arranged in a casual circle invite people to talk with each other. It says, "We are here to listen and respond to each other — and to learn together." If you are the leader, simply be sure to sit where you can have eye contact with each person.

Promptness counts. Time is as valuable to many people as money. If the group runs late (because of a late start), these people will feel as robbed as if you had picked their pockets. So, unless you have mutual agreement, begin and end on time.

Involve everyone. Group learning works best if everyone participates more or less equally. If you are a natural *talker*, pause before you enter the conversation. Then ask a quiet person what he or she thinks. If you are a natural *listener*, don't hesitate to jump into the discussion. Others will benefit from your thoughts but only if you speak them. If you are the *leader*, be careful not to dominate the session. Of course, you will have thought about the study ahead of time, but don't assume that people are present just to hear you—as flattering as that may feel. Instead, help group members to make their own discoveries. Ask the questions, but insert your own ideas only as they are needed to fill gaps.

Pace the study. The questions for each session are designed to last about one hour. Early questions form the framework for later discussion, so don't rush by so quickly that you miss valuable foundation. Later questions, however, often speak of the here and now. So don't dawdle so long at the beginning that you leave no time to "get personal." While the leader must take responsibility for timing the flow of questions, it is the job of each person in the group to assist in keeping the study moving at an even pace.

Pray for each other—together, and alone. Then watch God's hand at work in all of your lives.

Notice that each session includes the following features:
Session Topic—a brief statement summarizing the session.
Community Builder—an activity to get acquainted with the session topic and/or with each other.
Questions—a list of questions to encourage individual or group discovery and application.
Prayer Focus—suggestions for turning one's learning into prayer.
Optional Activities—supplemental ideas that will enhance the study.
Assignment—activities or preparation to complete prior to the next session.

One

Choose the Living God

Session Topic: Only God is intrinsically worthy of our worship and devotion.

Community Builder *(Choose One)*
1. See if you can name all Ten Commandments in the order they are given in Scripture. Refer to Exodus 20 to see how you did.
2. When and how did you first hear of the Ten Commandments (a sermon, Sunday School, your parents, a friend)? What was your reaction to them?

Discovery Questions
1. Hybels states that his aim is to show Christians that the Ten Commandments are still important for us today (p. 8). Why are these commands still relevant?
2. The first four commandments teach us how we are to relate to God. Review these commands as recorded in Exodus 20:1-11. How would you summarize the features that ought to characterize our relationship to God.
3. Why did God give us the first commandment? After coming up with your own ideas, refer to the reasons Hybels gives on pages 9–13.
4. Why is it actually in your best interest to believe and observe the first commandment? Read Psalm 115:3-8 and form your own paraphrase of these verses.

5. What person or thing do you find yourself thinking about in a quiet moment of free time? Why?
6. Consider where you spend your time, money, and energy in a normal day. What does this say about your purpose? About who you are trying to impress?
7. If you were to stand before God today to account for the things or people you made major priorities in life, how would you explain to Him your choices?
8. Hybels says that the person who obeys the first commandment wants to pursue God's will with a passion (p. 17). How are you *intentionally* seeking to make God's will your ultimate goal? Likewise, in what areas of your life have you let other "gods" compete for your allegiance?
9. What will it take for you to relinquish the person or thing that is obstructing you from total devotion to God? (Examples: greater trust in God's provision for your life, a better understanding of His love for you, etc.) What can you do about this?
10. What are some tangible ways that you can make God the object of your greatest affection?

Prayer Focus
- Read Job 38 aloud.
- Listen to what God says about Himself to Job.
- Allow 2-3 minutes of silence to reflect on the passage and your reaction to it.
- End the prayer time by offering praises to God in short sentence prayers. Thank God for who He is and how the truth of this first commandment means fullness of life for you.

Optional Activities
1. Begin your personal prayer time each day by affirming God's worthiness to receive your total devotion. You might say something like: "I come to you today, Lord, with my joys and concerns because only You have ears to hear my prayers and wisdom to answer them."

2. Write the words of Exodus 20:3 on a 3 x 5 card and place it where you will see it often. This is a way of reminding yourself that God deserves your rapt attention and that you need to trust in Him alone for the cares of your life.

Assignment

1. If you do not already keep a journal, begin one this week. Start keeping a record of your insights concerning the Ten Commandments. Each week focus on the particular commandment you have studied. Make journaling a regular part of your devotional time.
2. Read chapter 2 of *Laws of the Heart*.
3. Memorize Exodus 20:3.

Two

Don't Settle for Shadows

Session Topic: The reality of God transcends all images and ideas we can possibly conceive of Him.

Community Builder *(Choose One)*
1. On a religious continuum (highly sacramental traditions being on the far left of the spectrum and traditions which renounce all use of imagery representing the far right), where would you place yourself, and why?
2. How do you conceive of God? For example, what does God "look like" to you? Explain your answer.

Discovery Questions
1. Read Exodus 20:4-6. Hybels says that God does not want us to make images of Him because no one image can adequately reflect God's nature in all its fullness (p. 21). What do you think about "aids" to worship? Are all images "idols"?
2. The author notes that conceptions of Christ are subject to change over time. (For example, depictions of Christ in the '60s differed from those of the '90s.) What does the fact that human depictions of God change tell you about their usefulness?
3. Read John 4:21-24. What does it mean to worship God "in Spirit and in truth"?
4. How can images actually *prevent* spiritual and truthful worship?

5. Christians can worship God anywhere—on top of a mountain, while driving the car, on a walk at the beach. In view of this, what do you think about the use of certain places or items such as a sanctuary, stained glass windows, or incense to enhance your ability to worship God?

6. The problem with images, says Hybels, is that they present only one aspect of God's character. On pages 22–23, he refers to the seductive danger of Aaron's molded golden calf. He says that the calf pictured God's power, but not His holiness. How do Christ's parables (word pictures of a single aspect of the kingdom of God) differ from the danger presented by the golden calf?

7. What is the difference between thinking about an aspect of God and *fashioning a representation* of that aspect?

8. We all have a tendency to favor certain aspects of God's character and neglect others. Hybels notes that it is easier for us to try to change God than to conform to His will (p. 28). Why is this the case?

9. One way Christianity is distinct from all other religions is that God, through the words of the Old Testament prophets and through the Incarnation of Christ, has revealed to us *how* we are to think about Him—since we would have no other way to grasp One who is completely different from us. How can you better use Scripture to help you conceive of God?

10. What is the right use of the images given in the Bible, and when can those images become idolatrous?

11. List some ways that you can gain a *balanced* understanding of God—one that does not slip into idolatry but promotes your obedience to the second commandment? After coming up with your own answers, compare with those of Hybels on page 26, paragraphs 1 and 2.

Prayer Focus
• Take time to confess to God any misrepresentations of Him you have been cultivating.

- Ask the Holy Spirit to help you understand God's nature more fully as you meditate on Scripture's revelation of Him.
- End your prayer time by naming aloud some of the images of God provided in Scripture, thereby affirming His true character. You might pray: "Lord Jesus, we thank You that You are the Good Shepherd who. . . ."

Optional Activities
1. In your personal Bible study this week, look at the various images of God given in Scripture. (Most Bibles provide this kind of information for your reference.) Record your insights into God's character and nature in your prayer journal.
2. Walk through your home and your place of worship with an eye for images that might mislead in what they communicate about God. Consider what you can and ought to do to better obey the second commandment.

Assignment
1. Record your insights about the second commandment in your prayer journal.
2. Read chapter 3 of *Laws of the Heart*.
3. Memorize Exodus 20:4.
4. Ask a volunteer to research the names of God in Scripture to share during the next session. (See *The New International Standard Bible Encyclopedia*, *New Bible Dictionary*, or *Zondervan Pictorial Bible Encyclopedia* under "God, names of.")

Three

Turn Profanity into Praise

Session Topic: The name of God expresses His being and His holiness.

Community Builder *(Choose One)*
1. What does your name mean? What impact has the meaning of your name had on your life?
2. Read Exodus 20:7 in several different translations:

    NIV: "You shall not misuse the name of the LORD your God."

    NASB: "You shall not take the name of the LORD your God in vain."

    NRSV: "You shall not make wrongful use of the name of the LORD your God."

    Based on the various nuances reflected in these sample translations, come up with your own paraphrase of the third commandment.

Discovery Questions
1. Read Genesis 17:4-5 and 32:28. Why did God change the names of these people?
2. Read Hosea 1:3-9 and Matthew 1:21. How did God use the names of these people for a purpose?
3. How is God's name regarded in the Bible? (Ask the person who volunteered last week to research the names given to God to share his or her findings.)

4. "Every time we utter God's name, or sing it, we must do so thoughtfully," Hybels wrote on page 32. What would be your greatest difficulty in following this standard?

5. Why is it wrong to misuse God's name?

6. What are some reasons why people dishonor God's name? After coming up with your own list, confer with the reasons Hybels gives on pages 35–41.

7. Luke 6:45 summarizes why people dishonor God's name when it says, "For out of the overflow of his heart his mouth speaks." What does this mean?

8. Paul, in Colossians 3:17, exhorts Christians to strive to please God in *everything* they say. Should there then be any difference between how you use God's name and other things that you say, or are they all somehow related? Explain your answer.

9. What are some ways you misuse God's name both directly (as in active rebellion) and indirectly (as in ignorance)?

10. In the Lord's Prayer (Matthew 6:9) Jesus instructs His disciples to "hallow" God's name. Make a list of some practical ways that you can hallow God's name. Refer to Hybels' suggestions (pp. 37–39) after coming up with your own ideas. Which of these is a reasonable next step in your walk with Christ?

Prayer Focus
● Read 2 Timothy 2:11-13.
● Confess your sins against God's name, asking for His Spirit to change you.
● Thank Him that, as we desire to be more like Him, He remains faithful to us because we are His.

Optional Activities
1. Choose a mature Christian friend and ask him or her to hold you accountable to make and to keep God's name holy in the fullest sense of this commandment to be pure in speech.

2. Make it a regular part of your prayer time to ascribe to God some of the names given to Him in the Bible. You might begin your time of prayer by saying something like: "O God, You are the *Creator* of the universe and the Sustainer of all living things. . . ."

Assignment

1. Record your insights into the third commandment in your prayer journal.
2. Read chapter 4 of *Laws of the Heart*.
3. Memorize Exodus 20:7.

Four

Follow the Maintenance Schedule

Session Topic: God has established the day of rest as a time of physical, emotional, and spiritual refreshment for His people.

Community Builder *(Choose One)*
1. Share one of your favorite ways to unwind. Why is it so relaxing?
2. How did you grow up observing the Sabbath. Was it a day just like any other day, or was it somehow made distinct? How?

Discovery Questions
1. What are some things that you regularly maintain (car, house/apartment, etc.)? What are some of the tangible (e.g. fewer repairs) as well as intangible benefits (e.g. peace of mind) that you enjoy because of your regular care?
2. It is sometimes easier to maintain material possessions, like cars or houses, than things less measurable, like ourselves or our relationships. How would you rate yourself as to how well you "maintain" yourself? (Consider diet, regular exercise, friendships, etc.)
3. What happens to you when you don't take time to rest on a regular basis? Be specific.

4. Read Exodus 20:8-11. Hybels believes that God elaborates on the fourth commandment because He wants to be perfectly clear about our need for rest? Why do we have to be *commanded* to rest?

5. What kind of person needs a Sabbath? (Do you think that *everyone* needs to rest from work or only people who are less productive or less motivated?) Do you think that you should take a Sabbath rest from your work even when you don't feel particularly tired? Explain.

6. Read Mark 2:27 and Hebrews 4:9-11. According to these verses, what is the purpose of Sabbath?

7. Read Genesis 2:1-3, Exodus 23:12, and Isaiah 58:13-14. Based on the teachings of these sample verses, what principles should guide you in determining how to spend your day of rest?

8. Hybels mentions examples of professions that require employees to work on Sundays. If you must work on Sunday, what are some things you can do to get the rest you need? How can you meet your need (and obligation) for corporate worship?

9. One reason for Sabbath is for us to join with other believers to worship God. According to Hebrews 10:25, worship with other believers also provides support and encouragement in faith. How are you making worship with other Christians an integral part of your day of rest? How would you like to improve your personal worship during these times?

10. Hybels points out that there is more to life than work; there is the worship of God. In view of your day-to-day decisions, what would your family and friends say that you really believe about regular rest and worship?

Prayer Focus
- Reread aloud Exodus 20:8-11.
- Take time to praise God that He knows that we are frail and dependent creatures and has remembered our physical limi-

tations by commanding us to rest on a regular basis and be refreshed by worshiping Him.
- Ask the Holy Spirit to enable you to live a balanced life — one marked by obedience in work as well as rest.

Optional Activities

1. Examine you own practice of this commandment to take regular rest. Make a list of some specific ways you can make your Sabbath more restful and worshipful? Begin to put these ideas into practice this week. Record in your prayer journal the impact you observe your new choices making on your ability to love God and others.
2. Interview someone who seems to demonstrate rest in God. Ask for their "secret." Record your insights in your prayer journal.

Assignment

1. Journal some of your current thinking about the fourth commandment.
2. Read chapter 5 of *Laws of the Heart*.
3. Memorize Exodus 20:8.

Five

Fulfill the Cycle of Love

Session Topic: God's Commandments include the right ordering of family relationships.

Community Builder *(Choose One)*
1. Hybels notes that the home is the birthplace of our values. How did your mother and father demonstrate (either positively or negatively) the value of "honor" to each other? How has their example impacted your understanding of the concept of honor?
2. Based on your own family experience, why do you think God gave us a command to honor our parents?

Discovery Questions
1. Read Exodus 20:12. What do you think it means to "honor" your parents?
2. Why do you think this commandment is placed at the beginning of the commands concerning our relationships with others?
3. Read Matthew 15:3-9. Jesus makes it clear that true love for God is demonstrated by how we treat others—in this case our parents. What was wrong with the way the Pharisees observed the fifth commandment? What are some ways that we too might dishonor our parents?
4. Some people think that this commandment requires children (no matter how old) to do whatever their parents say.

What do you think? Is honoring the same as obeying? Explain.

5. Read Matthew 10:32-38. If your parents ask you to do something that you know to be against biblical teaching, how can you say "no" in a way that honors them? Give an example.

6. Hybels offers examples of how honoring your parents is different depending on whether you are still a child under their care or whether you are an adult living independently. Refer to Hybels' suggestions on pages 59–63 for general principles, as well as his summary of how to apply this commandment in the final two paragraphs of the chapter. In view of these, what do you think should characterize your treatment of parents when you are a child vs. when you become an adult?

7. Read 1 Timothy 5:3-4, 8. What principles does this text teach to children of aging parents? What are some practical ways that you could carry out that responsibility? How can you honor a parent who has died?

8. Paul says that you should honor your parents in order that "it may go well with you" (Ephesians 6:1-3). What is the "it" he is referring to? (See also Exodus 20:12.)

9. Read Philippians 2:14. What is one specific situation where you could contribute to family harmony by obeying this command?

10. If one or both of your parents are not believers, what are some ways that you can better demonstrate Christ's love for them through your words and actions?

11. In view of the biblical passages you have examined here, how does your attitude toward your father and mother measure up to the intent of the fifth commandment?

Prayer Focus
- Pray for your parents: their spiritual and physical well-being.
- Confess (without making excuses for) any negligent behavior or thoughts on your part in obeying God's command to honor your parents.

● Ask the Holy Spirit for wisdom and sensitivity to know *how* to honor your parents more fully and genuinely.

Optional Activities

1. Make a list of things you can do to show your parents honor in ways that are meaningful to them. These can be one-time acts or on-going items. Determine to fulfill several items on your list during the course of the next few months.
2. Write a letter of appreciation to your parents, listing specific memories or reasons why you are thankful for their example. This may not be easy if your family life was marked by strife, abuse, divorce, or death. If that was your experience, perhaps you could write a letter that you will not send but that gives you the opportunity to try to be faithful to God's command in the midst of a difficult situation.

Assignment

1. Record your insights into the fifth commandment in your prayer journal.
2. Read chapter 6 of *Laws of the Heart*.
3. Memorize Exodus 20:12.

Six

Destroy the Killer in You

Session Topic: The sixth commandment speaks to the root of the spirit of violence and all its manifestations.

Community Builder *(Choose One)*
1. Share an experience when you were on the receiving end of a "killer's" words. What was its effect on you?
2. Name a famous person in history, other than Christ, who you think has modeled obedience to this commandment? Explain your answer.

Discovery Questions
1. Read Exodus 20:13 and Matthew 5:21-22. Why does Jesus make a parallel between physical violence and verbal violence? What does He say will be the fate of both?
2. Besides cold-blooded killing, what other acts of violence are probably included in this prohibition against "murder"? (Form your own observations, then refer to Hybels' suggestions beginning on page 67.)
3. What actually is "killed" when you misuse the weapon of your mouth?
4. Why is this kind of murder just as heinous in God's eyes as actually killing someone with a knife or a gun?
5. Read James 3:9-12. What is James saying about the one who professes to love God, yet does not love people who are made in God's image?

6. Hybels speaks of "Chicago-style" murder, "surburban-style" murder, and "religious-style" murder. What does he mean by each? (See pages 64, 67, and 69.)

7. In what ways is each of these "murders" a violation of the sixth command?

8. Every day the news brings reports of the sufferings of the world. These can overwhelm us to the point that we can become immobilized by enormous problems and our own inability to solve them. But when we know of someone's need *and it is within our power to help* but we don't, Hybels says that we are guilty of "religious-style" murder — murder by neglect or apathy. Do you agree? Explain your answer.

9. Read Matthew 25:31-46. Why do we often resent our responsibility to care for the needy? (What suspicions do we harbor about the people we are trying to help? What excuses do we give ourselves?)

10. What does Jesus mean when he says that when we feed the hungry person and clothe the one who is naked we are actually doing these to *Him*?

11. If you are going to take seriously the implications of the sixth commandment, what will change in your own actions and words? Be specific.

Prayer Focus
• Read aloud the prayer of St. Francis:

Lord, make me an instrument of Your peace.
Where there is hatred, let me sow love;
where there is injury, pardon;
where there is doubt, faith;
where there is despair, hope;
where there is darkness, light;
where there is sadness, joy.

• Ask the Holy Spirit, who dwells in you and empowers you to obey God's commands, to make you sensitive to the power of your words.

● Invite Him to remind you of the price Jesus paid to buy your salvation so that you can be more aware of the common need for mercy toward one another.

Optional Activities

1. Take time this week to reflect on your treatment of others. Make a list of those you have harmed with your words or neglected with your actions. Confess your sins to the Lord and, like David in Psalm 51, ask God to cleanse your heart from these forms of murder.

2. Meditate on James 3 this week in your daily devotional time. Record your insights in your prayer journal.

Assignment

1. Record your insights into the sixth commandment in your prayer journal.

2. Read chapter 7 of *Laws of the Heart*.

3. Memorize Exodus 20:13.

Seven
Keep Pleasure Undefiled

Session Topic: God wants to safeguard the sanctity of sex within marriage.

Community Builder *(Choose One)*
1. Name the last movie you saw. What perspective toward sex did that movie promote?
2. Read Exodus 20:14 and Matthew 5:27-30. Come up with a working definition of "adultery."

Discovery Questions
1. The pressure to conform to the will of the majority can be intense or subtle. Share an instance where you allowed others to influence an ethical choice and why you did so.
2. Sometimes it's easier to try to reason a way out of following God's will (Adam blamed Eve for his disobedience and Eve blamed the serpent for hers). List some ways we try to excuse wrong thinking and behavior instead of taking personal responsibility?
3. Hybels says Scripture seems to indicate that God created human sexuality primarily for pleasure and secondarily for the purpose of procreation (p. 73). What do you think?
4. Since God has designed sex to be an expression of love, why is it not OK to have sex with someone you really love prior to marriage? After coming up with your own ideas, confer with Hybels' arguments on pages 75 and 79-81.

5. What hope and help would you offer a Christian who felt guilt about past sexual sins?
6. In view of Matthew 5:27-30, do you think that it is all right to view sexually explicit films or magazines if you're married? Explain your answer.
7. What is it about sexual intimacy that makes it such a powerful instrument for pleasure or pain?
8. Hybels says: "The sexual dimension of marriage often can be viewed as a barometer of the level of tension or harmony that exists in other areas of the marriage" (p. 76). Why is that the case?
9. If you are married, what are some specific ways you can affirm your commitment to be faithful to your spouse? (Refer to Hybels' book [pp. 77–78] for general guidelines.)
10. If you are not currently married, what are some specific ways you can affirm your commitment to be faithful to the Lord as well as to a possible future spouse?
11. Our culture actively promotes and cultivates sexual promiscuity. Make a list of ways that you can maintain biblical perspective and practice concerning sex in the midst of this pressure.

Prayer Focus
● Read aloud John 14:15.
● Ask the Lord to forgive you for dwelling on impure thoughts or behaving in an "adulterous" manner.
● Confess your need for God's grace and mercy to follow His commands.
● Express your thanks to Christ for His death on the cross which makes it possible for you to experience forgiveness for your sins and to live a life *with* God instead of apart from Him.

Optional Activities
1. Reflect on the perspective toward sexuality that you were raised with. Was the attitude permissive, repressive, or rela-

tively balanced? Think about some of the reasons behind this perspective. Record your insights in your prayer journal.

2. If you are married, ask yourself: "What am I doing now to establish a lifetime of sexual pleasure with my spouse alone?" Create an opportunity to communicate with your spouse how you can better satisfy each other's sexual interests.

Assignment

1. Record your insights on the seventh commandment in your prayer journal.
2. Read chapter 8 of *Laws of the Heart*.
3. Memorize Exodus 20:14.

Eight

Acquire by the Rules

Session Topic: God entrusts us with personal property acquired through work and gifts; stealing violates that trust.

Community Builder (Choose One)

1. Share an experience when you had something you valued stolen from you? How did it make you feel and why?
2. Share an instance where you were tempted to take something that wasn't yours but chose not to (this could be something tangible, like a basketball, or intangible, like an idea). Why did you choose not to steal?

Group Discovery Questions

1. Read Exodus 20:15. Hybels discusses three categories of stealing which the Bible condemns: seizure (Luke 10:25-37), deception (Proverbs 20:23), and fraud (Mark 12:13-17). What are some modern examples of each of these categories of stealing?
2. Why is stealing such an evil thing?
3. What does the act of stealing say about the thief?
4. What are some ways that people steal today but don't call it "stealing"? (Examples: bringing home office supplies from work for personal use, not declaring all income earned on tax submissions.) Why are these practices considered acceptable?
5. Proverbs 20:23 says God detests "differing weights." In

what two or three ways could you conduct your business or personal relationships more equitably?

6. The Bible teaches that certain means of acquiring are acceptable: diligent labor (Ephesians 4:28), investment (Matthew 25:14-30), and faithful prayer (Matthew 7:7-11). What makes these means legitimate?

7. Do you think that it is all right to *enjoy* the possessions you gain through hard work or by gift? Explain your answer.

8. When does enjoyment of possessions become idolatrous?

9. Read Matthew 6:19-20 and Luke 12:16-21. Hybels says that we store up "treasures in heaven" each time we use the resources God has given us to accomplish His will in the world (p. 86). What are some specific ways you can be "rich toward God" and thereby build up treasures in heaven?

10. Like the rich man in the parable, your "barn" can be overflowing but your soul empty. It is much easier to be consumed with building our own kingdoms and forget about building God's eternal kingdom. What are some ways that you can balance the need to work for a living and the call to work for eternal purposes?

11. God wants us to ask Him for things. James 4:3 is a caution about *how* to make our requests to God. How would you like this passage to impact your patterns of prayer?

Prayer Focus
- Read aloud Matthew 16:26 and take a minute to meditate on its meaning.
- Confess your sin to God.
- Ask him to strengthen you to obey His commandment not to steal in all its various forms.

Optional Activities
1. Make a list of everything you have "borrowed" from someone and promised to return but haven't (the neighbor's ladder, office supplies from work, etc.). Then make a covenant

between yourself and God to return everything on your list to its proper owner by the end of the month.
2. Meditate this week on Psalm 24:1, James 1:17, and Genesis 1:27-30. Record your insights in your prayer journal.

Assignment
1. Record your insights into the eighth commandment in your prayer journal.
2. Read chapter 9 of *Laws of the Heart*.
3. Memorize Exodus 20:15.

Nine

Hold to the Truth

Session Topic: God is Truth; any distortion of truth is abhorrent to Him.

Community Builder *(Choose One)*
1. Tell about a time that you remember lying about something. What were the circumstances and why did you lie? How did you feel later?
2. What is one way you personally take care to be truthful, especially when those around you are not concerned to act with integrity?

Group Discovery Questions
1. Read Exodus 20:16. What does it mean to "bear false witness" (NASB) or "give false testimony" (NIV)? You might consult a dictionary for a fuller range of meaning.
2. What circumstances tempt you to lie? Survey Hybels' comments on pages 98–100. What forces does he see behind these temptations?
3. The account of Adam and Eve's fall from grace in Genesis 3:8-13 illustrates our tendency to hide our sin. Why is it sometimes easier to cover our tracks with a lie than to tell the truth?
4. Read Genesis 2:17 and 3:1, 4-5 concerning how Satan distorted God's truth in order to deceive Adam and Eve. Jesus calls Satan the "father of lies" (John 8:44). What does

this name tell you about Satan?

5. In John 14:6 Jesus claims to be the truth. The very essence of God's nature is truth. What are some implications of this reality? (Example: God cannot tolerate dishonesty.)

6. Hybels notes that there are two subtle forms of lying that often go unchecked: distortion and exaggeration. What examples of distortion and exaggeration have you witnessed?

7. Is it always wrong to lie? Explain your answer.

8. Read Romans 7:14-25. Every one of us is tempted at times to mask our deceit. What does the passage in Romans teach you about the process of becoming a more truthful person?

9. Hybels observes that our society minimizes the seriousness of lying and conditions us to accept dishonesty as a way of life (p. 100). How then should you expect others to react when you strive to be honest?

10. If your family and close friends were asked to say how honest they thought you were, what would they say?

11. The Bible says over and over that we are to be lovers of truth and that this truth is found in the Bible (2 Timothy 2:15). Make a list of some specific ways you can cultivate a love for the truth? Be creative.

Prayer Focus

- Give thanks to God that He Himself is truth and that to know Him is to know truth.
- Knowing that dishonesty grieves God's heart, confess the times you have been careless in the way you handled the truth or were intentionally deceitful.
- Ask the Holy Spirit, the "Spirit of Truth," to bless you as you take steps to grow as a lover of truth.

Optional Activities

1. Make a list of people you remember having lied to in the past. Resolve to apologize, either in person or in writing, to at least one person on your list. This may be extremely

uncomfortable, but be encouraged that you are pleasing God in your effort to become a more truthful person.

2. Meditate on these verses concerning "truth": Psalm 119:160; John 8:32; Romans 1:25; Philippians 1:18. Record your insights about these passages in your prayer journal.

Assignment

1. Record your insights into the ninth commandment in your prayer journal.
2. Read chapter 10 of *Laws of the Heart*.
3. Memorize Exodus 20:16.

Ten

Crave Contentment

Session Topic: Coveting has wide-ranging effects on those who covet and on their relationships with God and other people.

Community Builder (*Choose One*)
1. Share an instance when you wanted someone else's job, spouse, car, etc. Were you aware, at that time, that you were coveting?
2. What is your greatest passion in life? (Hybels uses the example of his father's consuming interest in motorcycles.)

Group Discovery Questions
1. Read Exodus 20:17. What does it mean to "covet" something or someone? You might refer to the dictionary's definition.
2. What are some ways that our society encourages you to covet?
3. Hybels notes that the advertising industry pushes us to possess things and people (pp. 110–111). What are the repeated and subtle messages *behind* many ad campaigns?
4. How might you be causing people (whether they are employees, children, spouse, friends) to covet by the way you motivate them? (Example: you want your high school child to study more so you say to him, "Good grades, good college, good job, nice house. It all goes together. So study up!")

5. Read Ecclesiastes 4:4. How can this observation challenge you to rethink the way you conduct your business and the way you relate to others? Be specific.

6. Not all incentive programs are bad — it is those that produce a fixation that are wrong. What are some ways you can motivate people without manipulating them and thereby causing them to covet? Come up with a real-life scenario.

7. What is your idea of the "good life"?

8. When you catch yourself coveting another's wealth, status, job, personality, what is your coveting revealing about you? After making your own observations, refer to Hybels' two insights on pages 113–114.

9. What are specific ways that you can allow Scripture to have a more profound impact on your purchases?

10. We often hear about a person's "right" to certain possessions. These rights may give people a sense of dignity. But when we act like we have a *right* to have certain things or to be *like* someone else we are, in effect, telling God that He owes us. What, if anything, do you think God owes you?

11. Consider the story of Job. Job seemed to have it all: children, a home, servants, land, livestock. But when news came that everything had been destroyed and every person dear to him killed, what was his reaction? He worshiped God! (Job 1:21) Job seemed to know exactly where his "wealth" came from and who was the ultimate owner. How would you respond if something similar happened to you? What does your response tell you about your understanding of God and His relationship to your possessions?

Prayer Focus
- Read Luke 10:18-20 aloud.
- Meditate on how your relationship with the living God changes emphasis from what you *do* to who you *are* in Him.
- End your time of prayer by reading Job 1:21 aloud. Give thanks to God for its liberating truth.

Optional Activities
1. Make a list of all the things and people God has entrusted to your care. With each item you list, ask yourself whether you are being a good steward of the items God has given you. Having reviewed in this study the biblical attitude concerning "possessions," determine ways to address those areas where you notice an unbiblical attitude in yourself.
2. In your prayer time this week, meditate on the teachings found in Colossians 3:1-4 and Philippians 4:11-12.

Assignment
1. Record your insights on the tenth commandment in your prayer journal.
2. Memorize Exodus 20:17.
3. Read through the entries in your journal. Give thanks to God for this opportunity to know Him better and learn how to serve Him more faithfully.